Walking Home
Journey Toward Self-Healing

Renée E. Schmachtenberger Tijerina

SUNRISE
PRESS

ISBN: 979-8-9933133-3-7 (paperback)
ISBN: 979-8-9933133-1-3 (hardcover)
ISBN: 979-8-9933133-2-0 (ebook)

To my entire family, my friends, and the strangers who
gave me love and support every step of the way:
I wouldn't be here today without you.

To the caregivers: You are the heroes and angels of this
world. I see you. You matter. You make this life
possible.

To all the health-care providers: Thank you for the
sacrifices you make to take care of us. To each of you
who gives love, care, time, and truly listens to each
patient: Please take care of yourself too.

If you can't fly, then run. If you can't run, then walk. If you can't walk, then crawl, but whatever you do, you have to keep moving forward.

—Martin Luther King Jr.

Table of Contents

Before You Begin

I have lived and died several times in my lifetime. I walk with grief, keep my heart open with gratitude, and reflect on each life. Many people have encouraged me to write my story—surviving cancer, navigating life with a physical disability, and creating a meaningful life afterward—but for a long time, it never felt right. Part of that was because I needed to process and come to terms with my experiences. I've done the work—and continue to do the work—to heal, to grow, and to make peace with my journey. I am still learning and stumbling. I am stronger in new ways now. After everything, I have found the words and the courage to tell my story.

I wanted to set expectations for this book before you begin. The intent of this book is to help inspire you on your journey—whether you are just beginning, are somewhere in the middle, are nearing the end, or haven't even started yet. I want to encourage you to keep taking one more step, especially in those moments when moving forward feels impossible. Throughout this book I share snippets of my own life and my healing experience. My hope is that by sharing my life and my process navigating it, I can inspire you on your own unique journey. At times, working on yourself and experiencing the heartaches of life can feel isolating, difficult, and exhausting. This book is here to help you feel less alone and more connected. Your journey will be different from mine, and how you heal will be a different process, but we are walking in the same direction—forward.

This is a hybrid of a book and a journal. I invite you to reflect on what you read. At the end of each chapter I have included reflection questions, called "Fieldwork Reflections," to help you reflect. You may be asking why I chose to name these as such. I believe that when you experience life in all its glory, you are out in the field, learning lessons. These lessons can come quickly, so writing them down helps you remember and reflect on them later. I have incorporated blank pages between each chapter for you to write down your thoughts and ideas. I have also included extra pages at the end of the book if you need more space. Don't stop at just the reflection questions—if another thought comes to you while reading, write it down. On my own healing journey, writing down my thoughts has helped me sort through the jumbled array of ideas, feelings, and questions that pop into my head.

I intentionally made this book small and light so that you can throw it in your bag or carry it in your hands while you move through life. You never know when life is going to send you some new inspiration or when you'll need space to write down an intense feeling or thought. In my own journey I am often waiting—waiting for a doctor, a test result, or a call back—stuck with my thoughts swimming in my head, or I am just bored. In those times, I have often wished I'd brought something to read or had somewhere to reflect on my thoughts. In those times, reach for the book.

Take what you need from this book. Skip around. Reflect. Make your own meaning. Some things may resonate now and others later. Talk it over with a friend or a stranger. You might discover they are going through something similar, or they may inspire you to look at life in a different light. This is coming from an introvert who does not love talking to strangers. I despise small talk. In my life I get "nudges"—a push from God, the universe, or whatever you believe in—telling me to talk and connect with certain strangers I've encountered on my life journey. When I follow these nudges, I gain inspiration and a deeper understanding of life and humanity, and I meet an incredible human being along the way.

My Why

Before you start your reading and reflecting out in the "field," I'll share my why. My why in life is to motivate others to pursue their goals and rise above their challenges so that they can live a life that exceeds their dreams. I want to inspire people to not be debilitated by their disabilities and misfortunes. Life is both difficult and beautiful, sometimes all at once. The journey becomes easier when you know you're not alone, when you learn that others have climbed the mountain before you. I hope your life exceeds your dreams. This life is yours; you're stronger than you think. Take one more step.

Meaning Behind the Title

For those of you curious about the title *Walking Home*, the title had gone through a couple of changes until this version came to me in the middle of the night. I remembered that when I was sick, I often listened to the song "Home" by Michael Bublé. At sixteen I assigned that song my own meaning: I saw it as a song to my old self before cancer and the new self I was learning how to live with. For many years I struggled to accept my new life and just wanted to go back home to my old self. I didn't want to go through the treatments, side effects, or surgeries; I wanted my old life. There were times I also wanted to go home to heaven when I was horribly sick.

Some of the lyrics stood out to me. I cursed and hated my body for getting sick, for not moving the way I wanted it to, for limiting my everyday abilities. Those thoughts were hurtful and hindered my ability to accept myself, but the song helped me appreciate my self-worth. It also emphasized how lucky I had been—for all the support and help I had, for being able to get all the treatment and ultimately surviving. But I still wanted to go back home to my old self. The song was particularly relevant when I was diagnosed and my life was flipped upside down—my old life was completely gone. I was doing great in high school, had a wonderful group of friends, and was excelling in sports, and overnight that life was gone.

The song ends with an assurance that it will all be all right—and it was. It took time, and on some days it was hard to believe, but ultimately everything turned out more than all right for me. After years and years of working on myself, not giving up, processing the events in my life, accepting my body and my leg's abilities, I came back home to myself. I was able to return and sink back into my "home," feel safe in my own body, accept all that was and wasn't my life. I came home and created the life that was meant for me.

Perspective

Throughout this book I bring up my strengths and how they affect my life. I want to give some context for the idea of strengths and how I discovered mine. Before 2025, if you had asked me, "What are your strengths?" I probably would have stared back at you, unsure how to respond. I didn't know my strengths—but I could easily list my weaknesses. After my cancer diagnosis I became hyper-focused on what I lacked, constantly trying to improve my weaknesses. Eventually I realized it was time for a new perspective because my self-confidence was low.

In January 2025 I met with one of my mentors to discuss my desire to expand my knowledge to further enhance my skill set as an individual life coach. She encouraged me to take the Gallup-Certified CliftonStrengths Coach certification course. CliftonStrengths is a research-based assessment designed to help people identify their natural talents and turn them into strengths. The assessment, a series of 177 timed questions that measure your talents, ranks thirty-four talent themes that highlight your top strengths. Gallup founder Don Clifton defines talents as "naturally recurring patterns of thought, feeling, or behavior." Instead of focusing on fixing weaknesses, CliftonStrengths emphasizes maximizing what you do well naturally.

Once you've completed the assessment, you receive a personalized ranking of all thirty-four strength themes, with the top five being your strongest natural abilities. These strengths influence how you connect or work with others, make decisions, and approach challenges.

As I read my report, I realized I had always known these things about myself but had never recognized and intentionally used these talents as strengths. Learning about my top themes—Relator, Learner, Achiever, Empathy, and Intellection—transformed how I saw myself and gave me valuable insight about what contributes to making me who I am. For so long I focused on weaknesses, but now I could see how my strengths showed up in my daily life. My Relator strength has allowed me to build strong, authentic bonds with those I devote my time to. My Learner and Intellection strengths fuel my curiosity and love of school and learning about life. My Empathy strength helps me understand emotions and connect deeply with others, and my Achiever strength pushes me to keep going, even when life gets difficult.

Understanding all thirty-four strengths helped me make sense of my world. It provided the "why" behind my actions and beliefs. Shifting my focus from weaknesses to strengths gave me confidence and self-acceptance. I learned how talents can be nurtured and refined to create a strength. I stopped trying to force myself to improve things that didn't come naturally to me; instead, I shifted my focus to improving my natural, unique strengths. By changing my tactic, I felt like I was going with the grain instead of against it, which made accepting and embracing myself easier.

We all have unique, powerful strengths. Discover them. Build on them. Let them guide you to your best self. Lean on them in difficult moments. Let them help you take one more step when you feel like you can't.

Fieldwork Reflection: What are your strengths? How can you use them to help guide you through life? If you're unsure of your strengths, I invite you to find a CliftonStrengths coach who can help guide you through the assessment and understand your results.

FIELDWORK REFLECTIONS	DATE

INSIGHTS	NOTES

NEXT STEPS

FIELDWORK REFLECTIONS	DATE

ADDITIONAL NOTES

FIELDWORK REFLECTIONS	DATE

ADDITIONAL NOTES

FIELDWORK REFLECTIONS	DATE

ADDITIONAL NOTES

Part I:
Knocked Off My Path

Sometimes you have to start over to
find your true path in life

DIAGNOSIS

*You have been assigned this mountain so that you can
show others it can be moved.*

—*Mel Robbins*

In May 2007, at the age of fifteen, I started to experience pain under my right knee when I was doing my routine early-morning run. I tried to shake it off, thinking I must have pushed it too hard during a workout. As the weeks went on I felt more unstable and weaker around my knee. I noticed that my knee was warm to the touch, with a small lump. In my gut I knew something was seriously wrong. Despite the discomfort and worry, I carried on with life, not wanting to slow down. That summer I went to California to stay with family and spend time with them. I walked down to the beach every day. I tried to run on the beach, but the pain worsened.

I decided to share my symptoms with my mom and my aunt, a pediatrician. My aunt encouraged me to have an X-ray done as soon as I returned home to Texas. At the end of June 2007, I had an appointment with my pediatrician. The doctor advised it was nothing but a minor sports injury. As he walked out I stared at my mom and asked her to please tell him I need an X-ray. She stepped out and spoke to him; he agreed to her request. A few hours after the X-ray procedure, we received a call from the doctor advising us to come in right away to do an MRI. My heart sank—I knew something was terribly wrong.

Days before my sixteenth birthday I received the news. I was diagnosed with stage I osteosarcoma in my right tibia and needed to see a pediatric oncologist as soon as possible. My family had no history of osteosarcoma. I was blindsided, facing a reality I never imagined. Two things ran through my mind: *What do we need to do to beat this?* and *I need to tell my best friend I won't be able to attend her birthday party since I'll be getting chemo.* I didn't allow myself to feel fear—all I knew was I had to survive.

I wasn't a stranger to cancer, but I was too young to grasp its true impact. In elementary school, in the first grade, I had a dear school friend who had cancer. I witnessed what cancer did to her: She lost her hair, had low energy, missed school, and lost her life several years later. I kept my friend in my heart, and I was determined to give it my all and fight till I had nothing left.

In early July, I met with my pediatric oncologist. He had my treatment plan ready to go, since he had received all the tests from my primary care doctor. The doctor explained my treatment plan: a biopsy, then several rounds of different types of chemotherapy, then surgery, and then more chemotherapy. The information was a lot to take in and overwhelming to process. I didn't have the time to slow down to sit with my emotions. I felt numb. I didn't know what feelings to process first: nervousness, sadness, fear, anger, grief . . . The best I could do was have tunnel vision on the treatment plan.

Each treatment phase or procedure was a stepping stone toward the finish line. I didn't know if I would walk across that line on my two legs, but I knew I'd cross it even if I had to drag myself. I'm a person who thrives on accomplishing things—whether it's a school or work task or personal development, it brings me joy. Now, with house chores, I'm not as driven, but I will get it done eventually. For the most part, you can give me a task and I'm going to get it done, which is the exact energy I channeled to prep myself on this journey. On July 13, 2007, I underwent an open biopsy of my right proximal tibia. Shortly after, I had a port-a-cath, or implanted port, placed on the left side of my chest. Everything was happening incredibly fast. The only option in my mind was to keep moving, never slow down, and endure whatever I needed to in order to survive.

When you receive any type of diagnosis or devastating news, it feels like the world has stopped, when in reality the world keeps moving no matter what is going on in your life. The world kept going for my family and me. That same summer, before I received my cancer diagnosis, my parents broke the news to my siblings and me that they were getting a divorce and that my dad was moving out. Spoiler: They got back together and remarried years later. A few days before I received my cancer diagnosis, my family received news that my young cousin had died and that one of my aunts was in remission from breast cancer. Some years are unbearably heartbreaking, but in between the heartbreak and devastation, there are breaks of good news. Over the next couple of years, my family and I experienced highs and lows. We leaned on each other and supported each other where we could. It was still a struggle, but we kept going.

I could probably write a whole book about the things my family has done for me throughout my entire life. For the sake of brevity, I'll mention only a few. My parents set aside their differences. Despite being in the middle of a divorce, my dad moved back in to be there for me during my cancer journey. My parents also relocated my bedroom downstairs by reconfiguring the dining room. They didn't want me climbing the stairs with my weak leg, especially not when I was having a bad day due to treatment. My grandparents, who were over seventy, lived a little less than two miles away and would visit me every day to check on me. On days when my grandfather couldn't drive, they would walk to my parents' house with freshly prepared oatmeal for breakfast and my grandmother's famous homemade Mexican rice for lunch. She always made enough for all of us to eat.

One of my eleven aunts, who lived in another state, would fly down on surgery days to be with me and support my parents to make sure they could take breaks when needed. She also helped keep hope alive and made sure each day felt special to me even when I felt horrible. She set up a mini Christmas tree made of silver aluminum tinsel in my hospital room—even though it wasn't close to December—which we took home once I was discharged. Each week she sent me a small gift with an encouraging note. She made each day feel like Christmas. When I faced losing my hair, another aunt stepped in, sending a surprise box of colorful scarves with a note: "Kick ass."

At times I needed blood transfusions. When this happened, immediate and extended family members would donate blood—even the ones who were terrified of needles. Other family members always checked in on me, helped support fundraisers for me, cooked food for us, and were a shoulder for my parents to lean on. Every time I was in the hospital, I was never alone. Even when I was sleeping, someone was always there—my dad, mom, aunt, or brother would be sitting or sleeping in the hospital room chair.

Each of these things has meant the world to me. The way I gave thanks was by giving it my all each day. Some days it was 100 percent; other days it was 60 percent. But either way, I always gave whatever energy I had to keep going.

My experience with chemotherapy was horrible, although I've never heard anyone say they enjoyed the experience. I told my parents I felt like I made a deal with the devil. I had a chance to live, but I lose almost everything: my hair, taste buds, appetite, skin color, immune system, blood count, muscle, mental stability, immediate life goals . . . the list goes on. During one of my rounds of chemotherapy, I experienced a severe allergic reaction that led to renal and liver failure. I vividly remember feeling like I was burning from the inside out at that moment. I felt like my internal organs were on fire.

I remember trying to rip the IV out of my arm, wanting the chemo to stop going into my veins.

I was rushed to the ICU, where I remained for over a month, undergoing dialysis. It was one of the scariest moments of my journey. The days in the ICU blurred together—I remember having lucid nightmares of being left inside a burning hospital to die, a side effect of the morphine. Other than those nightmares, I don't remember much, but I do know my family stayed by my side, praying I would pull through.

Recovery was slow and painful, but during that time, I received love from strangers, friends, and family. One of my best nurses surprised me on her day off and visited me to deliver lunch, which included a milkshake. Apparently, I had been talking about milkshakes in my dreams. Even my pediatric oncologist found ways to make me smile, lending me his prized tea set and encouraging me to have a tea party with my friends. The same compassion showed up outside the hospital too. Friends from my school and my dad's work coordinated fundraisers to help with the medical bills. Despite facing one of my toughest times and fighting for my life, I received the most beautiful love and care, which helped me keep moving forward. These people taught me that you can still find joy even under horrible circumstances.

After recovering from my near-death experience, I began another round of chemotherapy. Thankfully, I didn't experience any more allergic reactions. At the same time, we faced the next big step in my treatment plan— planning surgery on my leg. A local doctor insisted I had no choice, that amputation was the only option. I was fortunate to have a family who believed otherwise and insisted there were other possibilities. My mother refused to accept his answer, and her doubt pushed her to search until she found another doctor. She discovered a team at MD Anderson in Houston, Texas, that included doctors who specialized in the type of cancer I had.

At sixteen I had to decide on a surgery option for myself. Depending on how you looked at my situation, you might have thought I was given the luxury of choice, or you might have concluded I had been burdened with the responsibility of choosing. Just months earlier, the most important decisions in my world revolved around school activities and ice cream flavors. Suddenly I was choosing between surgeries that would determine the rest of my life.

My mother took the first appointment available, and we made plans to drive up to Houston. I met with a team of doctors, and they advised me that I had three surgery options to choose from. I was stunned. I had options when I was told there were none. Without hesitation we transferred my care to MD Anderson. My family made many sacrifices for me to complete my chemo treatment in Houston and have the surgeons at MD Anderson operate on my leg.

Option one was amputation, and options two and three were similar: I could keep my leg and have my tibia, knee, and a portion of my femur replaced with either titanium or donor bone from a cadaver.

I experienced severe analysis paralysis, knowing whatever decision I made would affect the rest of my life. I researched and asked my doctors questions about the surgery process, recovery time, side effects, and quality-of-life outcomes. Little data was available, but I worked with what I had. What I wish I had done was look for support groups for people who had had similar surgeries of amputation or endoprosthetic reconstruction. They would have had data based on firsthand experience for me. I went through the pros and cons of each surgery, and none of the options really seemed like a "winning" choice.

What I really wanted was to keep my leg and have the cancer vanish. My parents said they couldn't make the choice for me, that I had to decide for myself. It was coming down to the wire, and I had to choose. I went to my room, sat on my bed, and held my leg. I stared at the lump on my tibia. I was still and tried to clear all the noise from my head to find a straight path to my answer. I was terrified of the idea of waking up after surgery and no longer having my leg. I was also devastated knowing that if I chose to keep my leg, I would lose my ability to run and participate in any high-impact sports, something I lived and breathed for. I decided it was time to find a new love and passion, and I opted for the titanium.

On surgery day, they marked my leg and wrote in big letters "THIS ONE." I thought, *How unlucky and unfortunate it would be to do surgery on the wrong leg,* and with that I said "I love you" to my parents and was put under anesthesia.

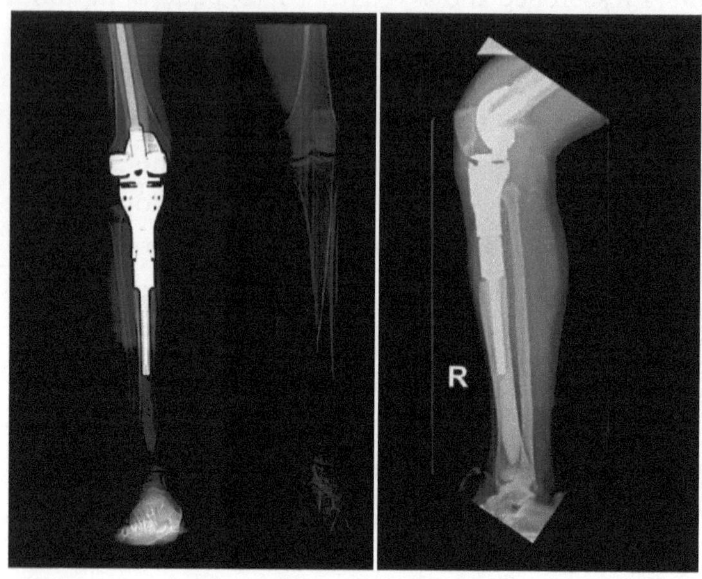

X-ray imaging of my right femur, knee, and tibia taken in 2024. My right leg was surgically treated for osteosarcoma of the right tibia on December 18, 2007—the surgery was a reconstruction using a proximal tibial endoprosthesis with associated constrained rotary knee joint. Revision surgery was performed on November 30, 2023, including resurfacing of the patella and exchange of bushings.

After several hours of surgery, when I awoke, the first thing I asked for in a raspy voice was water. My throat felt dryer than a desert and like pieces of glass were stuck in there. My lips were also starting to crack. The nurses in the recovery room were not responding to this request. I believe they did this because they didn't want to tell me no. My mother was soon by my side and asked what I wanted. She pleaded with the nurses that I needed water. They advised I would have to wait to drink water to ensure I would not aspirate it into my lungs. They didn't want to take the risk. My mother stayed on the nurses like a hawk and kept asking when I could have water. She wanted to make sure my request was not forgotten. Eventually they gave me ice chips and told me to only suck on the ice and slowly let it melt.

Once I had that pain relieved, I finally felt the searing pain in my back from the epidural catheter. I could feel it around my spine. It felt like it was constricting me. I demanded that it be taken out. Yes, I am a very demanding person when I am in pain. The doctor advised me that the catheter was helping control the pain in my leg. I countered that it was causing me immense pain and that I'd rather suck up my leg pain instead of feeling pain in my spine. We debated for a while and discussed the pros and cons, which eventually led them to take it out. I slowly felt the pain creeping into my leg, but I was determined that I would be able to handle it.

Several hours after recovering from the surgery, the physical therapist came and told me it was time to get moving. They warned me about this, that they would want me moving as soon as possible to help the mobility of the leg and the healing process. The first step was getting out of bed, then eventually doing a lap around the nurses' station.

Slowly I inched myself over toward the edge of the bed in my hospital gown, willing my leg to hang off the edge. It felt like my leg weighed a hundred pounds, like it was dead weight. The pain shot up, sending a zap to my brain. I gritted my teeth, my eyes teared up, and I death-gripped the walker, hoisting myself up. I was determined to keep the pain at bay because I didn't want an I-told-you-so lesson about the pain. I doubt anyone would have done that, but still, the thought was there. I finally got myself standing up, and I'm pretty sure I was mooning the nurses. I felt the blood rush down to my leg, making the bandages tighten, pulling at the fresh stitches, making me feel faint. I couldn't hold back my cries, and I yelped at the insurmountable pain I was experiencing. I was starting to sweat. The physical therapist said that was enough for now and he would return in a few hours to try again.

Little by little I kept taking more steps, and I tried again and again to make my lap. I was absolutely exhausted, mentally and physically. I refused to take strong pain pills because I hated the numerous side effects. I stuck to nonsteroidal anti-inflammatory drugs and acetaminophen, which helped only so much. My main motivator was that I wanted to get home in time for Christmas. The surgeons and physical therapists made a deal with me: If I could successfully complete one lap around the station, I could be discharged the day before Christmas. Needless to say, I made it home for Christmas.

My father rolled my wheelchair next to the glittering Christmas tree, and with my dog in my lap, I got to spend time with my family. It was time to celebrate and recover in my own home. My recovery at home consisted of me needing support showering, going to the bathroom, changing my wound dressing, getting dressed, getting food from the kitchen, and finding clothes to fit around my giant brace (loose, breezy dresses were great, but during winter, those convertible pants, the ones you zip off into shorts, were fantastic). I also needed regular transportation to attend physical therapy.

After a month or so of this routine, I started to go stir-crazy and needed a change of scenery. My parents could tell that I was getting antsy and asked where I wanted to go. I told them I wanted to go to the mall to get ice cream and see the new styles of clothes that were rolling out for the next season. Before we went out we had my blood levels checked to ensure my immune system was strong enough to go out. I received the all clear and explored the mall in my wheelchair with my mom and aunt. The trip gave me the boost of joy I needed to keep going strong on my recovery journey. This season of my life was made possible by the endless support of my family.

The road to recovery was a long one. I restored my health to the best it could be after several rounds of chemo and a scare involving a spot found on one of my lungs that fortunately disappeared after a few more rounds of chemo, completed countless physical therapy sessions to learn how to walk again with titanium in my leg, and tried to keep up with schoolwork to ensure I'd graduate on time. I did what I could and healed with haste, ready to keep moving forward. In hindsight, I also needed to heal my mental health—my whole family needed to heal. However, once again, we handled what we could at our capacity. We were all just trying to stay afloat.

Before rushing back into my "normal" world, my doctors encouraged me to make a wish with the Make-A-Wish Foundation. I wasn't familiar with the foundation, but what my doctors told me was to dream big. Believe me, I dreamed big. It had been a wish of mine since the third grade to go to Australia to see the Great Barrier Reef and the Sydney Opera House. This wish started when a guest came to my elementary school with animals from Australia and shared stories of that magical land. I was enamored and knew I would have to go there one day. Well, here was my chance. When I told the foundation my wish, the representatives fell silent. They were surprised I didn't want to go to Disney. After talking it over, they told me they could make it happen. A few months later, I packed my bags, boarded the plane, and was so thrilled I barely closed my eyes during the twenty-hour flight.

I was in a dream. The colors, the animals, the food, the kind people—it was all beyond my expectations. Our first stop was Cairns, where we took a boat ride and snorkeled on the Great Barrier Reef, surrounded by fish, sharks, and brilliant coral. I wasn't even afraid of the sharks. I told myself I'd made it this far with my leg; I would be okay.

The next stop was Sydney to see the Sydney Opera House. The moment the magnificent building came into view, it took my breath away and I cried. I couldn't believe it. I survived the cancer, got to walk on my own legs with titanium, and have one of my long-time dreams come true. From then on, I knew I wanted to keep surprising myself: to exceed my own expectations, to defy the odds, and to celebrate both the big and the small moments in life. Each moment I am given is a gift.

I am now thirty-three years old. I'm still here, alive with titanium in my right leg, in a life that I cherish. It's not perfect, but it's beyond what I imagined for myself in the best possible way. I have the most incredible family, a place to call home, and a career that supports my dreams and wellness. Throughout this life, I have experienced pain, setbacks, anxiety, depression, dissociation, happiness, excitement, joy, and miracles.

Undergoing treatment—enduring chemo and surgeries—took a toll on both my mental and physical health. I have been cancer free for seventeen years now, but the journey didn't end when treatment stopped. At the age of sixteen I held the belief that life gives you only one major hardship to overcome. I had no idea how much more was in store for me. Since my survivorship, I have been diagnosed with hyperthyroidism, undergone a thyroidectomy, continued to manage ulcerative colitis, and managed the challenges with my leg.

In 2017, hyperthyroidism swept in with a whirlwind of symptoms: increased anxiety, a racing heart, hair loss, insatiable hunger, weight gain, feeling constantly hot, and mood swings. Yet I didn't receive a diagnosis until a few months later, during a trip to California, when severe food poisoning landed me in the hospital. I had been sick in the bathroom for hours, unable to keep anything down. I was starting to feel faint, and I knew the symptoms were beyond food poisoning at that point. My husband and I took an Uber to the hospital since we didn't have a rental car. I was praying I wouldn't be sick in the poor rideshare man's car.

Once I was checked into the hospital, the doctors ran tests and said not only did I have severe food poisoning but I also potentially had an underlying condition that was making it worse. They wanted me to stay for another day, but I told them I couldn't because my flight was leaving the next morning. They stared at me and then made a deal with me. They said I had to contact my local doctor and request an appointment immediately to figure out what condition I had. I promised I would, and they sent me on the way with strong medication to ensure I would not get sick on the plane.

Lo and behold, after running blood tests and going over the symptoms I had been experiencing for the past several months, I was diagnosed with hyperthyroidism and was referred to an endocrinologist for treatment. I was put on medication, which I had a severe allergic reaction to that involved full-body hives. Due to the medication not being an option for me, I had to have surgery to remove my thyroid, and I'll be on medication for the rest of my life. In truth, I wish I had had more time to process my diagnosis and research hyperthyroidism and the different ways to treat it, but I was a few months out from my wedding and was just trying to feel better.

Several years later, in 2023 I started to get sick again; I began a journey with ulcerative colitis. I had been experiencing symptoms off and on. I noticed I was becoming a lot more sensitive to certain foods, which led me to spend hours in the bathroom. When I wasn't having a reaction to food, I noticed I was no longer going to the bathroom regularly anymore. I was also starting to lose weight. I was proactive this time and sought medical advice. But the doctor brushed me off and said I probably just need antibiotics. That didn't sit right with me. I knew there was something wrong beyond a minor illness. I consulted with another doctor, who took the time to listen as I shared my whole story. His willingness to truly hear me led him to refer me to a gastroenterologist.

After several tests—blood work, stool tests, and a colonoscopy—I was diagnosed with ulcerative colitis. I asked my doctor many questions about treatment options, natural and medical; the ins and outs of the disease; and what websites to review to learn more. I wanted to tread slowly before I jumped into treatment with medication due to my history. My doctor and I discussed my concerns, and he said he was open to me trying the natural way (changing my diet and eliminating inflammatory foods) for a few months. He told me that if diet changes didn't work, I would need medication to help heal my intestines, which were bleeding at the time. Changing my diet made things better, but not enough, so eventually I had to begin taking medication. I am still actively on this journey, but because of my past experience in the medical world, I feel equipped to handle this condition.

During that time, between 2020 and 2024, I also experienced a miscarriage, postpartum anxiety, and depression, which I discuss in further detail later. Each challenge tested me in new ways, reminding me that survival isn't just about overcoming one battle—it's about accepting the challenge, continuing to fight, and persevering through whatever comes next.

Fieldwork Reflection: What was the most difficult choice you have had to make in your life? How did you come to your decision?

The first several times I've shared my story I cried, because it is remarkable I have survived. It reminds me where I have come from and that I can handle any future challenges. Have you ever shared your story? If not, who can you share it with? If you have, what did you learn about yourself?

FIELDWORK REFLECTIONS	DATE

INSIGHTS	NOTES

NEXT STEPS

FIELDWORK REFLECTIONS	DATE

ADDITIONAL NOTES

FIELDWORK REFLECTIONS	DATE

ADDITIONAL NOTES

FIELDWORK REFLECTIONS	DATE

ADDITIONAL NOTES

IDENTITY

The spirit never dies.

—Dr. Edith Edgar

There was a time when I believed the girl I was before cancer died. The girl who played soccer and ran track. The girl who was fearless and spontaneous. The girl who could take a hit and bounce back up. I felt that losing the ability to run and participate in high-impact activities made me an incomplete person. I was ashamed of and embarrassed about myself. I didn't want people to see my scars. I could only see my incomplete, imperfect self. My goals were hyper-focused on how I could improve my weaknesses, and I couldn't see my strengths. I buried my old self, telling myself there was no way I could ever be her again. I had dreams that I was that girl again, running freely; I always woke up in tears. Her memory always seemed to linger no matter how hard I tried to leave her in the past.

That is, until one day when I was invited to look at things with a new perspective—with the idea that the spirit never dies and is always part of you. I was listening to a podcast that featured Dr. Edith Edgar, and she was talking about the spirit. That's when it clicked. It was like someone turned on a light for me. All my journaling and healing work and the books I had read in the past about the spirit never dying, all those valuable lessons finally clicked on for me and made sense. When I reflect on that now, I believe I was ready to receive that message at that moment. I probably had heard it many times in the past, but at that moment, I was ready and open to receive that message.

I paused the podcast and reflected on what helped me survive cancer and my other diagnoses and how I made my life meaningful after surviving. It was my tenacious, fearless spirit, the one that was dominant before cancer. The exact spirit I was trying to bury and get rid of. It was the courageous and tough spirit that braved chemo and surgery, learned how to walk again, and made countless hard decisions that would affect the quality of my life and determine whether I would continue to live. I sobbed knowing that she had been there all along, that she was not dead and that I got to keep her. I may not be able to run anymore, but my spirit continues to persevere and carry me through the marathon of trials in my life. Without that tenacious spirit, I wouldn't be where I am today.

Fieldwork Reflection: Reflect on your past self. What do you want to say to them? What do they say to you? How is your past self still part of you now?

FIELDWORK REFLECTIONS	DATE

INSIGHTS	NOTES

NEXT STEPS

FIELDWORK REFLECTIONS	DATE

ADDITIONAL NOTES

FIELDWORK REFLECTIONS	DATE

ADDITIONAL NOTES

FIELDWORK REFLECTIONS	DATE

ADDITIONAL NOTES

ADAPTABILITY

*When we are no longer able to change a situation, we
are challenged to change ourselves.*

—Viktor Frankl

If I had remained the exact same person I was before
cancer, I wouldn't be alive today. Year after year I have
had to adapt to the changes in my life. I now take time to
reflect on myself each year, identifying behaviors that no
longer serve me and determining which new behaviors
I'd like to integrate. Remaining static wouldn't have
allowed me to overcome the challenges I faced.

Before cancer I was dedicated to sports. I lived for it.
I loved waking up early and staying late after school to
practice soccer, track, or cross-country. I was silly and up
for most adventures—dance parties, road trips, dressing
up, and going to the mall. I enjoyed being with my friends
and loved school. Academics were not my primary focus.
I was not a straight-A student, but I loved learning and
competing with other students.

I asked some of my wonderful long-time friends who
knew me before cancer what kind of person I was back
then. They shared that things seemed to come easy to me.
I was social and had a big circle of friends. People
naturally gravitated toward me. They also mentioned that
I was a people pleaser, someone who didn't want to rock
the boat. My brother shared this: "Before cancer I saw a
goofy, thoughtful, happy-go-lucky girl who at times was

childlike. Your spirit had never been so broken as when your hair started to fall out. You were completely devastated the first time you had to shave your head. But over time you slowly became that goofy girl again. This time, though, you were goofy and took no one's crap. You learned not to take life for granted and to take care of those you love. You showed you were a fighter, and that never changed—it never will."

From my perspective, after cancer I became more serious and cautious and had a different outlook on life. I developed the belief that energy and time were precious. I was unsure how long my energy and health would last; therefore, I became selective about how I spent my time and with whom I spent it. This new outlook and way of living helped me be more intentional in how I spent my time and what friendships I devoted myself to. My intentionality was focused on family—being able to be with them and creating a life in which I could balance work and fun, which for me is traveling, experiencing new places, and spending time with loved ones. The downside of becoming more serious and cautious was that I was overthinking everything, highly on guard to make sure I wouldn't get hurt, trying to plan everything, and trying to control my world, which made it harder to have fun, be silly, and live in the moment.

For as long as I can remember, I have always experienced some anxiety, but it was manageable. For example, in elementary school, if my mom was even a minute late to pick me up after school, I would worry and imagine she had been in a car accident. I would go to the school office and ask that they call my mom to make sure she was okay. Don't ask me why I thought that—it was an irrational worry I had. However, after cancer my anxiety intensified and became harder to manage. As I grew older I spent a lot of time overthinking and anticipating how every little thing I did might affect my leg or whether I was even capable of participating in an activity. I became more self-conscious and worried about what others thought of me. I was insecure about how my hair and face looked. My face swelled and grew pale from all the chemo and the time I spent in the hospital. I had to figure out how to style a bald head and navigate the awkward growing-out phases afterward. I was embarrassed by my scar and usually covered my leg. I didn't want people to ask me about it. I didn't want their pity or to face the awkward silence after I told them what happened. As each year passed by, I started to accept myself a little more but still struggled with confidence and my identity after cancer.

About sixteen years post-cancer I realized it was time for another big shift and completely changed my lifestyle. I kept getting sick with different issues—thyroid and digestion problems—along with postpartum anxiety and depression. My anxiety and nervous system were stuck on high, in fight-or-flight mode; my body would shake even with minor injuries. I was becoming burned out and losing myself. I felt my light dimming. I knew this wasn't a sustainable way of life—I needed to change my way of life; otherwise, I knew I wouldn't survive.

It wasn't until after my son was born that I truly dedicated time and energy to healing myself. I am now someone who is calmer, moves through life at a slower pace, and has learned to manage my emotions and anxiety in a healthier way. While I still experience struggles, they are not as overwhelming as they once were. I worry far less about others' opinions. I learned that when I was constantly trying to be aware of everyone else's opinions and trying to read their minds, I was making myself small and self-conscious. It was exhausting, and I gained no benefit from that behavior; it only put me in a spiral of people-pleasing and created shallow relationships. I learned that if I showed up as my authentic self, I attracted people who accepted my whole self, quirks and all.

What I am still working on is being confident in my decisions and not asking for others' opinions on my potential life choices. I have to cut myself off midpoint sometimes and say never mind when I start asking for someone else's opinion. I know no one else can make a decision for me. I'm the one who has to live with the choices, not the people who give their opinion. We all have our own unique individual lives, and no two people will ever walk the same exact path, which is why only we can make our own decisions. I'm mindful of times when I do need to consult with others, when I'm trying to navigate a situation that I have zero experience in. I ask questions, do research, and ask for people's perspectives, but then I sit down with the information and ask myself what feels most right for me.

Working on my self-confidence has helped me move past analysis paralysis and focus my energy on what truly matters in my life, including prioritizing my health by eating well and moving my body regularly. Focusing on my health was only part of the foundation. Having the right people around me was just as essential. I have a small but close-knit circle of friends and an incredibly strong bond with my family. I go into greater detail about prioritizing my health and relationships later in this story.

These changes have helped me let go of the shame I once felt about my scars. When someone asks what happened, I confidently respond, "Cancer." Because I am proud—not just of surviving cancer, but of the life I have built since surviving it.

Fieldwork Reflection: Where do you feel stuck? What scars are you trying to hide? How might your life look if you could confidently show your scars?

FIELDWORK REFLECTIONS	DATE

INSIGHTS	NOTES

NEXT STEPS

FIELDWORK REFLECTIONS	DATE

ADDITIONAL NOTES

FIELDWORK REFLECTIONS	DATE

ADDITIONAL NOTES

FIELDWORK REFLECTIONS	DATE

ADDITIONAL NOTES

Part II:
Some Roads Have No Map

Moving forward when nothing
feels certain

THE UNKNOWN

When I look back on all these worries, I remember the story of the old man who said on his deathbed that he had had a lot of trouble in his life, most of which had never happened.

—Winston Churchill

At the follow-up appointment after my surgery, I asked how I would know when it was time to replace the titanium and other parts in my leg. "You'll know when it's time to replace your leg," my doctors told me. They explained that legs of my "type" typically last about ten years before needing to be replaced. They advised me not to run on it, to stick to low-impact exercise, and to maintain a healthy weight. Following these instructions would prolong the longevity of my leg. They said I would know when it was time for a revision surgery because I would experience pain and mobility issues.

Being me, I set an internal countdown in my head: ten years. I believed that by year ten I would be in pain and lose my ability to get around. As you can imagine, that looming deadline was not great for my mental health. As the ten-year mark approached, any pain or knee lockups that caused mobility issues felt like confirmation that the end was near for my original leg. The reality was that these issues were often caused by changes in the weather or overexertion from walking or working out.

Year ten arrived, and I was still doing relatively well. Year eleven rolled around, and I thought, *Okay, this is it. This is the year. Be prepared for surgery and all that comes with it.* Well, year eleven came and went. In the eleventh year, during my annual checkup at MD Anderson, I asked my doctor, "When will it be time for revision surgery?"

She looked at me and said, "Not anytime soon. Your cement and rods are all in great shape."

I was stunned. I had been so convinced that when the clock struck ten years, it would be time for my next surgery. Looking back, I realize that my sixteen-year-old brain must have misunderstood the doctors' statement for about ten years. They probably said *approximately* ten years, but I had taken it as an absolute fact.

I made it to sixteen years with my original titanium before needing to do any type of revision surgery, and even then only my knee needed a revision. Yes, revisions are not a walk in the park, but that was much better than having to replace a titanium tibia and a part of my femur. I asked the question again after my revision surgery: "How much longer do you think my tibia will hold up?"

The doctor replied, "Oh, you can make it last maybe ten, twenty, even thirty years. Just keep taking good care of it."

I was absolutely dumbfounded by that answer. From this experience, I learned a few lessons. First, the time people assign to approximations can vary widely. Second, it's important to ask detailed questions up front and write them down so I don't forget. I've also discovered the value of bringing someone with me to appointments so they can share their perspective on what was said. Still, asking questions doesn't come easy to me. It makes me feel vulnerable, because it reveals the emotions behind what I'm asking. An example of this type of question is "Can you tell what to expect regarding the durability of my leg? I am incredibly anxious, and I stay up at night worried that I'll need another surgery soon and that the experience will be painful." I learned that giving the why behind the question helps people understand where you are coming from and allows them to better tailor the answer for you. If someone doesn't know the answer, ask them who can answer the question for you or what resources can support you.

From the above example it's evident that nothing makes me more uncomfortable than the unknown, especially when it comes to my health. Thoughts of *What if it's this? What if it's that? Is it time for surgery?* will go through my mind a million miles a minute. My anxiety will increase, making my body shake and fouling my mood. The funny thing is that I just want to know what the problem is and when it will arise so I can make a game plan—both mentally and logistically. I'm confident that I can handle whatever comes my way. However, life doesn't work that way; I cannot predict or control the future. Life is unknown. We can try to plan all day, but as the saying goes, man plans, God laughs. Life's unpredictability can feel like a roller coaster, but I've learned to steady myself through prayer and to lean on my natural strengths. One of those strengths is being "restorative"—a quality that, as my CliftonStrengths report puts it, means I "love to solve problems. [My] ability to analyze a situation, identify potential shortcomings and modify as needed makes [me] powerful in times of difficulty and crisis."

I am powerful in times of crisis, but my weakness lies in waiting. Not knowing what the crisis or problem is makes me anxious. Patience and being present are two things I have actively worked on strengthening over the past year to help me cope with uncertainty. I have strengthened these skills through meditation. An excellent question I learned from the book *Ready, Set, Slow: How to Improve Your Energy, Health, and Relationships Through the Power of Slow* by Lee Holden is "Where are you?" This is followed up with "How do you know that's where you are?" Asking myself those questions brings me back to the present and reminds me where I am and to focus only on what's happening in front of me.

This practice helps me cope with the unknown and ground myself in the gift of now. The countless what-if scenarios I run through my head will never change the one outcome that is going to occur. The what-if scenarios actually make me feel worse and exhausted. My real life is happening in the present, yet I'm missing it by worrying about an unknown future. One example of this is when my leg hurts and I have difficulty walking. When that happens I worry that I'll have to go to Houston to have another surgery. I'd be away from my family and have to endure a long recovery process. I stress about that happening, and then I go one step further by trying to make a game plan for if that happens. However, from another perspective, all this worrying is costing me valuable time—time that could be spent being fully present with my family in my beautiful home right now. I still flow between the past, present, and future, but it's easier to pull myself to the present more frequently by being aware of my thoughts and grounding myself where my feet are.

Fieldwork Reflection: How does the unknown affect you? What helps you brave the unknown and keeps you grounded?

FIELDWORK REFLECTIONS	DATE

INSIGHTS	NOTES

NEXT STEPS

FIELDWORK REFLECTIONS	DATE

ADDITIONAL NOTES

FIELDWORK REFLECTIONS	DATE

ADDITIONAL NOTES

FIELDWORK REFLECTIONS	DATE

ADDITIONAL NOTES

EBB AND FLOW

Where you are now is not where you will always be.
Just keep on trying, and know that tomorrow really is
a new day.

—Jen Goodwin

We are always changing, little by little, like the phases of the moon. On my journey I've had to work through accepting that growing stronger and becoming weak again is part of my process. For approximately a year and two months after my first leg-revision surgery, I kept growing stronger and stronger. I started to develop muscle in my atrophied right quad. My gait improved, and I no longer had a limp. Every morning I woke up and planted my feet on the ground with no pain, my knee moving smoothly. I was disciplined and committed to my workout routine and physical therapy sessions until I started to feel pain in my right ankle.

I knew in my gut that this was the start of me slowing down. I asked others for their opinions on the pain, hoping I was wrong. However, I knew my body best and couldn't dismiss the fact that something in my ankle was strained. Despite this, I was determined to keep my routine and not slow down. I continued to exercise, modifying each movement whenever my ankle protested in pain. Eventually I had to stop and listen to my body when the pain didn't subside. It was time to rest and reset.

I would start the cycle again of giving my body time to heal and then starting physical therapy again.

I grow tired of the highs and lows with my leg and get frustrated with my health overall, but I've learned how to better cope with the low moments. In the past I would panic, and anxiety would take over. I could feel only my pain and drown in it on the inside. Now, after years of learning how to cope with pain and working through my anxieties, a low moment in my life is more manageable, and it no longer seems like the end is near. Many of my strengths have helped me. The ones that stand out are the Learner, Responsibility, and Empathy themes identified in the CliftonStrengths report.

The Learner strength shows up as a craving to learn more about myself and the world. I do this by reading and listening to podcasts and audiobooks to learn about new ideas or concepts about life, nature, the world, self-help, science, and fantasy. I apply the knowledge I gain to help me cope through tough times and be inspired by peoples' life journeys. Responsibility helps me stay committed to taking care of myself and my family. I know I must take care of my mental and physical health to be the best version of myself for them. When it comes to Empathy, I excel at having empathy for other people, yet I struggle with empathy for myself. I am my toughest critic, always expecting more from myself. I used to motivate myself with cruel words and little compassion, especially when it came to my health. After years of work through counseling, coaching, journaling, and other wellness practices, I'm learning how to have self-empathy and cultivate a kinder inner voice. I've accepted that my body is high maintenance and requires support in different ways at different times in my life. My job is to listen to it and help it. It's unrealistic to expect that my health will remain static and that I'll be able to continue doing the same things for the rest of my life. What's more realistic is expecting life to ebb and flow and to be able to respond with compassion and an open mind.

Fieldwork Reflection: How can you tend to your unique needs during this season of your life? What lessons are you discovering in the ebbs and flows of your life? How have you learned to be more patient with yourself?

FIELDWORK REFLECTIONS	DATE

INSIGHTS	NOTES

NEXT STEPS

FIELDWORK REFLECTIONS	DATE

ADDITIONAL NOTES

FIELDWORK REFLECTIONS	DATE

ADDITIONAL NOTES

FIELDWORK REFLECTIONS	DATE

ADDITIONAL NOTES

Part III:
The Courage to Ask

Learning to ask and receive

HELP

*"What is the bravest thing you've ever said?" asked the
boy.*

"Help," said the horse.

—*Charlie Mackesy,* The Boy, the Mole,
the Fox and the Horse

Asking for help did not come easy for me. I love to
be independent and do the damn thing myself. However,
my life has pushed me into many situations in which I
absolutely need to ask for help. I've also experienced
some hard lessons because of being too proud to ask for
help and trying to manage by myself. This normally
resulted in me getting hurt, which meant I needed even
more help. As someone with a physical disability, I
regularly need extra assistance and support with everyday
house chores and errands. Speaking the words to form a
sentence to ask for help used to pain me, frustrate me,
humble me, sadden me, because I wished I could do it
myself. But wishing life were different doesn't serve me;
if anything, it makes me feel worse.

Throughout my journey I've learned how to cope
with accepting what is. I've also realized what incredible
support I have from my loved ones, people who are
willing to give their time and energy to help me. They
don't keep score. They don't hold anything against me.
Without question, they show up.

As I reflect on this, it's no surprise my top strength is Relator. It's what I lean on, and it's what keeps my world going. My Relator strength shows up as my deep appreciation for close, trusting relationships. Having friends who truly know me means they understand when I go through seasons of life during which I need more help or accommodations in how we spend time together. They understand when I can't do activities that involve walking for a long time or stay at a hotel that doesn't have an elevator and requires me to climb several flights of stairs. They check in with me throughout the day to see how I'm feeling. They don't mind if they have to push me around in a wheelchair. They're always open to pivoting and making new plans so I can partake in the "adventures" with them. All these accommodations and the thoughtfulness without hesitation make it easy for me to speak up and ask for what I need.

I treasure my relationships. They improve my quality of life immensely. My understanding, patient friends have helped me feel more comfortable with asking for help in general—with receiving help from not only loved ones but also from strangers. I have learned to set aside my pride, because if I hadn't, I wouldn't be where I am today. There's always more than one way to look at something. Instead of being humiliated by my need to frequently ask for help, I'm grateful that I have loved ones who accept me as I am and make me feel comfortable enough to ask for help.

It takes both vulnerability and strength to ask for help. In addition to building those skills, I had to learn how to let go of control. When you ask for help, things won't always be done the way you would have done them. I've learned to bite my tongue because trying to micromanage often led to unnecessary bickering. At the end of the day, when you ask for help, you have to learn to accept that it may not be done the way you would have done it—but if it achieves the same result, that's what matters. Being kind to yourself and being kind to others when asking and receiving help makes the experience better for everyone.

Fieldwork Reflection: How comfortable are you asking for help? Reflect on a time when you did ask for help and it was successful. How might your life be different if you asked for more help?

FIELDWORK REFLECTIONS	DATE

INSIGHTS	NOTES

NEXT STEPS

FIELDWORK REFLECTIONS	DATE

ADDITIONAL NOTES

FIELDWORK REFLECTIONS	DATE

ADDITIONAL NOTES
75

FIELDWORK REFLECTIONS	DATE

ADDITIONAL NOTES

ACCESSIBILITY

We need to make every single thing accessible to every single person with a disability.

—Stevie Wonder

I stared at the long staircase leading to the restaurant, then turned my gaze to the winding maze that was the wheelchair ramp. Neither of them seemed appealing. My leg currently isn't in a state that requires a wheelchair, but when I'm faced with a long staircase or a long, winding path, the effort drains me. When I'm faced with accessibility issues it intimidates me and stresses me out. At the end of the day I just want to get inside the building and have a good time. I don't want to test out my leg's capability and deal with spasms or aches while I'm trying to be out having a good time with friends and family. Often I look up a restaurant beforehand to see what its access is like and whether the parking is close. If it's not accessible for my type of physical disability, I recommend that we go to another restaurant. Sometimes changing the restaurant or outing location isn't possible, and I just have to make the most of it and slowly go up one step at a time. Sometimes I have to sit out if it isn't possible for me. It's disheartening to face accessibility issues when you want to be out experiencing the world.

What I will say is this: These setbacks don't stop me from trying to leave the house and make a life beyond my home. It took me a couple of years, but I'm finally comfortable asking for wheelchair assistance at the airport. I can't even imagine trying to rush to a connecting flight or stand in those long TSA lines. I truly appreciate each person who assists me at the airport to make sure I have a positive and stress-free experience.

Having assistance makes a difference not only when I travel but also in the moments I share with my family while we're out exploring. We love going to zoos, theme parks, and botanical gardens, places that usually involve a lot of walking. I'm grateful that many of them offer electric or standard wheelchair rentals so I don't have to sit out when I get tired. There are seasons of my life when walking long distances isn't possible, and in those times using a wheelchair becomes essential.

I get many stares when I'm using an electric wheelchair because I don't look like someone with a disability. The reality is that many types of disabilities exist, some visible and others invisible—there's no certain way a person has to look. I've learned to let the stares and side-eyes roll off me and focus on enjoying myself with my friends and family. Other people's opinions don't change my reality, and I refuse to give them power over how I move through the world.

I still enjoy traveling, and because of my disability, I take time to research in advance and call ahead to ask about accessibility accommodations. There often are accommodations, or if there aren't any, some people will try to figure out some way to help you—you just have to ask. My hope for the world is that it becomes more accessible to people with all types of disabilities so that they can experience life and explore the world without barriers.

Fieldwork Reflection: What has held you back from exploring the world? Imagine if you boldly advocated for yourself—what would that look like?

FIELDWORK REFLECTIONS	DATE

INSIGHTS	NOTES

NEXT STEPS

FIELDWORK REFLECTIONS	DATE

ADDITIONAL NOTES

FIELDWORK REFLECTIONS	DATE

ADDITIONAL NOTES

FIELDWORK REFLECTIONS	DATE

ADDITIONAL NOTES

Part IV:
Beneath the Surface

Trusting the light will return

PARENTHOOD

In raising my children, I have lost my mind but found my soul.

—*Lisa T. Shepherd*

I met my now-husband in 2010, when I was eighteen and working a summer job at a local theme park as a loss prevention worker. This job involved me being undercover, monitoring guests and employees to make sure no one was stealing merchandise or pocketing money. If I did witness someone doing that, I needed to confront them and apprehend them. It was certainly a struggle to do my job when someone took off running when I caught them stealing. Yes, being in loss prevention probably wasn't the best choice for me when I couldn't even run. Luckily, I could always call for backup. I landed that job because it was the only option available at the theme park—my brother was a manager there, and we weren't allowed to work together. Don't ask me what possessed me to want to work at the theme park so badly. I just followed my gut, and I'm glad I did because it led me to meeting my husband.

On the first day of the job, I arrived so early that I had to wait outside the hall for my colleagues to arrive. My now-husband showed up next, and when I introduced myself to him, I knew he was my person. I felt it in my heart. He, though, took a little longer to come around. He claims he was playing hard to get (insert major eye roll). Our first date was at the lake, where he wanted to teach me how to wakeboard. I didn't think twice about my leg's limitations. I just wanted to spend time with him and try something new. That date is a testimony to how much that man liked me, because I am sure I wore his patience thin. Teaching me how to wakeboard resulted in me elbowing him in the nose multiple times. I'm surprised I didn't break it. Nonetheless, he didn't give up on me, and eventually he said, "Forget everything I told you—just hold on." Sure enough, on the next attempt I popped up and started wakeboarding. Sometimes life is like that: You have to clear your mind and hang on and trust you'll end up where you need to be. The rest, as they say, is history. We had our share of highs and lows, and our relationship was tested by being long-distance while I was away at school in Austin, Texas, but we made it through.

While I always knew I wanted to marry him, I was never the type of person who daydreamed about becoming a parent. It wasn't something I was opposed to, but it wasn't front and center in my mind either. Still, as our relationship grew serious, I made sure to tell him that the likelihood of me being able to have kids was slim due to all my cancer treatments. I've always been transparent with my husband about my health conditions. I wanted him to decide for himself if he wanted to share a life with me, knowing it would include big medical events and times when I would have to depend on him. Without hesitation he said he was staying in the relationship with me.

In 2017 I walked down the aisle in rain boots, because our wedding took place in the middle of Hurricane Harvey, a Category 4 hurricane. The wind was so powerful that the roof shook and swayed. Rain poured down in sheets. Our guests walked sideways to get into the building. Despite the threat, we were going to get married. The storm didn't stop us; it prepared us. The day was messy, loud, and unpredictable, just like life is. It was an honest start to our lives coming together, a clear sign that we would keep showing up for each other, no matter what hits.

A couple of years after we got married, we decided to go to the doctor to assess the condition of my ovaries and the true possibility of me having kids. The results showed that my reproductive system looked several years older than my age, with an egg count far lower than expected. Even so, we decided to try for a baby. I told myself that if a child wasn't in our future, we would focus on building a life together exploring the world and creating memories. In 2022, to our joy, our son was born.

But before his birth, in 2020, I experienced a heartbreaking miscarriage. This was during the COVID pandemic. I transitioned to working from home, but my husband was an essential worker, which meant he continued his work as usual. The precautions at this time affected many aspects of daily life, including my doctor appointments. Since I was pregnant, I had to be prescreened for COVID to make sure I wasn't sick, wear a mask, and go to the appointments alone. My husband had to miss the appointments, and while I shared the updates with him, it wasn't the same. I had earlier and more frequent appointments than usual because of my lack of a thyroid, among my other health issues. They had to keep checking my blood levels and adjusting my thyroid medication to make sure it was the right level to support my pregnancy. The hardest appointment was my seven-week appointment, when I was told they no longer heard a heartbeat.

When they broke the news to me, I sat in silence and nodded, listening to the instructions following the miscarriage. All I kept thinking was *I have to repeat all of this to my husband, and it's going to be excruciating for both of us.* You may be wondering why I didn't have a more dramatic reaction to the news I received. I was already expecting it—I was just waiting to hear it confirmed. A few days before my appointment, I had a vivid dream that I gave birth to my child and that a nurse placed her in my arms. Now bear with me here. Remember, this is a dream, but my child told me that she was leaving me and that she loved me. In the dream, I clenched her close to my chest and wept. When I awoke, I was crying and felt a pain in my abdomen. I knew my child had died at that moment, which is why I was only waiting for the confirmation at the doctor's appointment.

I grieved by writing poems, and I planted a sunflower garden in my backyard—an offering of light for every child lost to miscarriage. We didn't tell anyone about the pregnancy or the miscarriage, which made some conversations exceptionally upsetting. Well-meaning family members would ask us when we were having kids. Friends would tell us we would have the cutest child, then ask when we were planning to have kids. I had no response for these questions because I knew if I answered, I would cry or give a frank answer and blurt out, "I just had a miscarriage." I would just give my husband a look, and he would handle the conversation.

On a day when I felt isolated and lost in my grief, I found myself scrolling through Instagram, just one of the ways I was making it through. I stumbled on the account of one of my favorite chefs, who had shared her fertility and pregnancy journey, including several miscarriages. Without expecting a reply, I sent her a message to thank her for sharing her story and for helping me feel less alone. I even asked for her advice on handling the "when are you having kids" questions. To my surprise, she replied, saying she uses those moments to educate people on what is and isn't appropriate to ask about families and kids.

This exchange opened my eyes to the fact that asking people when they are having kids or why they don't have kids is an inappropriate question. I had never really given thought to these questions until I was the one on the receiving end and experiencing my own pregnancy challenges. You never know what someone is going through, and if they want to share their family plans with you, they'll do it when they're ready.

After a couple of weeks had passed, I finally felt comfortable telling some people about my miscarriage. I reached out to a dear friend who experienced miscarriages herself, and she listened with love and held space for me. That phone call will remain special to me for the rest of my life.

When I was pregnant for the second time, I was terrified that the pregnancy would also result in a miscarriage. My primary emotion at that time was anxiety. After several months of crashing waves of anxiety, my son and I both survived the pregnancy. Despite both my husband and me wanting and planning for a child, raising our son has been one of the most challenging and rewarding life experiences we have faced. It has also been one of the most emotional. The experience is filled with love, joy, and gratitude but also sadness, exhaustion, and frustration. For the first several months, my son wanted to eat almost every hour and couldn't sleep without being held, which meant we were extremely sleep deprived and I was overstimulated. We were both running on fumes, which caused both of us to be exceptionally irritable, and I cried easily.

We also had to learn how to navigate my son's severe allergy to our beloved dogs. Giving them up for adoption wasn't an option I wanted to entertain. My poor son was covered in hives from head to toe. I can get a little dramatic when stuff needs to be cleaned, and I knew I needed to rid the house of the allergens. I sent the dogs to be cleaned and had the house, air conditioning system, and ducts professionally cleaned. I also had a professional install a purifier in the AC and bought air purifiers for every room. To bring relief to my son, we quarantined the dogs in one section of the house and consulted an allergist for treatment options. Within a few days his hives started to clear up, and after several months he grew a tolerance to the dogs' allergens and their existence in the house. Ironically enough, my son is a cat person and not a fan of dogs. On several occasions he has requested that we get rid of the dogs. Full disclosure: The dogs spend most of the day lying around, ignoring my son, unless he leaves food out for them to steal. Can't win it all. We survived those months with the help of our family and by hearing our son's loving coos and giggles and taking in his sweet buttermilk pancake scent.

Being a parent with a disability affects not only me but also my entire family. As I navigated becoming a parent, I also had to be mindful of my leg and what it could tolerate. From being pregnant to giving birth to carrying my son in my arms, I had to be cognizant of how I was using my leg and how much stress I was putting it under. Facing those physical challenges pushed me to lean on my strengths of Restorative and Intellection. They show up in my life through my love of deep thinking and my passion for solving problems. They've taught me to approach challenges with curiosity rather than frustration, which has been essential in learning how to parent while caring for my leg. Even when my body has limits, my mind finds a way forward, constantly pushing me to think outside the box about how to stay active and present with my son. For example, my son loves running around and being active, yet running is not possible for me. I knew I had to think of another way I could play with my son. I created a game called "shadow monster," which involves dimming the lights and using a flashlight to create a shadow with my hands. The shadow chases my son around the house while I sit in a chair. It's one of his favorite games. I always keep other activities that I'm capable of, like playing with playdough or bubbles, building Lego, or even helping me cook, in my back pocket.

I've had to educate my son from an early age about my disability and what I'm capable of. One of the hardest lessons to date was me telling him I couldn't carry him anymore. By the time he was about eighteen months old, he was getting too heavy and too big for me to carry with my leg. He would beg and cry for me to pick him up, and it broke my heart every time. I grew tired of constantly telling him what I couldn't do, so I shifted the conversation to what I could do. I would tell him, "Mama can hold you on her lap." Focusing on what I could do created a more positive experience for both of us. This positive shift changed our daily interactions. It gave him comfort and it gave me confidence, and the feeling of inadequacy slowly began to lift.

As he grows older I'm discovering new challenges we have to navigate and find compromises for. He recently learned how to ride a bike, and he really wanted to go out and ride it. The problem was it was only me at home. I told him he had to stay close to me, that he couldn't go fast since I cannot run. Yes, of course in hindsight this was a horrible idea, but in the moment I felt comfortable, since it was only in our neighborhood and we know most of our neighbors. Well . . . how much can you expect of a three-year-old when it comes to remembering to stay close during the exhilarating experience of riding a bike? He took off, and I started to sweat, terrified that a driver wouldn't see him. I started to shout at him, and he ignored me. I felt myself getting faint, and I knew my legs couldn't carry me any faster. I felt utterly devastated and powerless. This scenario was completely out of my hands. Eventually he figured out I wasn't near him anymore, and he stopped for me. It was probably only a one-minute experience, but it felt like time stood still.

Needless to say, I don't take him on bike rides anymore. Now we stick to simple, calm walks together when it's just the two of us. My son and I are learning together how to navigate our relationship and are mindful of what my capabilities are. Becoming a parent has been continuously challenging and has made me truly face my disability and accept what I can and cannot do. Each day he inspires me to keep learning about myself and loving myself as I am. Being my son's parent is an unimaginable gift I didn't think was possible for me.

Fieldwork Reflection: What unexpected gifts are you giving to your child by showing up exactly how you are? How has parenting differed from what you expected? How have you adapted?

95

FIELDWORK REFLECTIONS	DATE

INSIGHTS	NOTES

NEXT STEPS

FIELDWORK REFLECTIONS	DATE

ADDITIONAL NOTES

FIELDWORK REFLECTIONS	DATE

ADDITIONAL NOTES

FIELDWORK REFLECTIONS	DATE

ADDITIONAL NOTES

FADING

*It is only in our darkest hours that we may discover the
true strength of the brilliant light within ourselves that
can never, ever, be dimmed.*

—Doe Zantamata

In August 2022 I fell into the deepest, darkest black hole. It happened subtly, quietly; little by little I was slipping into the cracks of darkness. It slowly started after I became pregnant again after my miscarriage. I was incredibly anxious about losing the baby, and it made it hard for me to enjoy the pregnancy. Full transparency—I was never the type of person who said, "I love being pregnant." I was inundated with anxious thoughts, constantly worrying that my baby might not survive. I tried to guard my heart by not getting too attached to the life growing inside of me. I was terrified that if I let myself love too deeply, I would be shattered all over again.

Despite my fears a miracle happened in January 2022: After I was in labor for more than twenty-two hours, which was made bearable by the support of my husband and our birth doula, my son arrived. Holding him in my arms was a surreal moment—all three of us had survived the pregnancy: myself, my leg, and my son. My husband's main job during labor was to be my leg's guard. He had to make sure no one tried to put me in a position that could potentially hurt my leg or tried to force my leg to bend more than was possible. On a good day, after I've stretched and ridden the stationary bike, my knee can bend a little over one hundred degrees. We were fortunate that the hospital had a birth doula available for us that day. She was our guardian, advocating for us and making sure we understood the full scope of any decisions we had to make during labor.

I thought giving birth would end the constant state of anxiety, but instead, it only intensified. On top of that I became increasingly irritable. I was overwhelmed with all the things I had to learn as a new parent. Online meetings were the only option at this time because the COVID precautions were still in force, but you can learn only so much on Zoom. I wanted to be the best parent for my son. It took a toll on me. At first I started to withdraw from my hobbies, telling myself I was too tired. Then it got harder to get out of bed unless it was for my son. Then the silence crept in, and I pulled away from the people who loved me the most. For months I had been experiencing high levels of anxiety, breastfeeding on demand around the clock, and barely getting any rest. I was utterly exhausted, mentally and physically.

Before I realized it, the world around me had gone dark. I couldn't find my way out. I couldn't even see a glimmer of light above me. But I refused to stop breastfeeding my son. I didn't care what it cost me. I truly believed that him having breast milk would protect his health. I wanted to lower the chances he would experience health issues. Honestly, I was terrified that my son would get cancer, even though my cancer wasn't hereditary. I felt that I owed it to him to sacrifice myself to ensure that I did everything I could to prevent him from getting sick. This irrational thought alone should've been a red flag to me and a sign that I needed to talk this through with a professional. In hindsight, I didn't have a healthy mindset. I know now that a baby being fed with love is best, whether it's formula or breast milk. I had a goal of breastfeeding him for a year and a half. I was so committed to that goal that I didn't realize I was losing myself and wasn't able to give my son the best version of myself.

When everything around me went dark, I thought I could help myself by using my previous coping techniques. None of them were working, and I was falling deeper into darkness. Weeks were passing by, and it was becoming harder to be happy and kind. I painted a mask on my face, pretending I was okay. The mask wasn't just for the people who visited our home; it was also a way to deceive myself. I wanted to believe that I was "okay" and not living in the darkness. I couldn't face myself. The only thing I could do was take care of my son, nothing else. I didn't want to talk to or see anyone, not my husband, not my closest friends. I wanted to curl up into a ball and cease to exist.

When I had the chance to sleep for a few hours, I couldn't. I decided to sit in the shower, and to my surprise I started to sob uncontrollably. I felt my heart shattering, my limbs going weak. I was at the bottom of a pit. I don't know how long I stayed in the shower. I couldn't get myself to step out, so I dragged myself out, whispering the words, "Help me." My husband came in and helped me up. I was shaking and told him I wanted to live for my son. I also knew I owed it to myself; I needed to live for me. I didn't come this far to give up. I told him I needed help as soon as possible. I went online and found a postpartum counselor with availability for the next morning. My husband held me through the couple of hours of sleep we could get.

It was then that my intense healing journey began. In addition to starting virtual counseling, I consulted with my son's pediatrician, and she encouraged me to slowly start weaning my son off breastfeeding to give myself relief. Outside of consulting medical professionals, I knew I also needed a creative outlet, somewhere to free my mind from anxieties, which prompted me to research art classes. I knew I needed to leave the house—I needed to allow my mind and body to breathe in a different space. I needed my world to be bigger than only taking care of my son. Creating art has always been something that has helped me express my feelings and get into a flow. I found a four-week pottery-wheel class that intrigued me. I decided to sign up. I didn't know anyone and didn't ask any of my friends to join me. I knew I needed a space just for me.

After the first day of class, I knew it was one of the best things I could have done for myself. During the two-hour class, I didn't have any anxious thoughts or stress about my baby (he was being cared for by people I trusted, which was a hurdle in and of itself). For those two hours I was me, and only me. I didn't have to fulfill the role of being a mother, a wife, or a daughter or wear any of the other hats I wore. I was incredibly focused on learning the techniques and creating pottery. I lost track of time. I forgot everything, except for what was right in front of me. My mind and soul needed that disconnection, a space to create. A space to start freeing my mind from the darkness of depression and anxiety.

This was difficult to share, but my hope is that after reading this you don't wait as long to get help. I believe that no matter how educated or trained you are in healing or therapy techniques, you can't do it alone. You don't have to be pre- or postpartum to experience anxiety or depression—it can happen to anyone at any time in life. Ask for and get support.

Fieldwork Reflection: When you start shifting away from your light, who can you reach out to for support? What resources are available to you?

FIELDWORK REFLECTIONS	DATE

INSIGHTS	NOTES

NEXT STEPS

FIELDWORK REFLECTIONS	DATE

ADDITIONAL NOTES

FIELDWORK REFLECTIONS	DATE

ADDITIONAL NOTES

FIELDWORK REFLECTIONS | DATE

ADDITIONAL NOTES

PARTNERSHIP

The greatest thing you'll ever learn is just to love and be loved in return. But sometimes love requires more than we think—more patience, more sacrifice, more understanding than we could have imagined.

—Unknown

"Accept what is. This is the situation we are in, and we are going to figure it out and make it work." That is a variation of something my husband has repeated to me many times throughout our relationship. One of the biggest struggles I've faced in our relationship is allowing him to be a caregiver to me, especially when he's already taking care of our son. I'm an empath, and I can feel my husband's tiredness, frustration, and sadness when he's overwhelmed from his caregiver roles. I see the daily sacrifices he makes for me and our son. Sometimes, when I get overwhelmed by the weight of his emotions and the sheer number of sacrifices he's made, I get frustrated too, and we end up bickering. It's not easy, but we've learned that we have to reset often and have hard, vulnerable conversations on how to move forward together.

There have been more times than I can count when I've been out of commission from leg pain, surgeries, or illness and he has stepped fully into the caregiver role. It's in those moments that guilt and shame, and the deep ache of wishing I could take care of myself, creep in.

When my husband sees this, he reminds me, "I knew what I was signing up for when I married you. I want to be with you, and I love you." If I'm honest, sometimes it's hard for me to believe him, but over the years I've gotten better at accepting the love and care he gives. Our relationship has taught me many lessons, but one of the most important has been learning how to receive love without conditions, without a scoreboard. Even so, learning to receive hasn't meant letting go of my need to contribute. It's critical for me to feel that I can offer something back, even when I'm the one needing care. I have an incredibly hard time just sitting back for weeks on end, allowing others to help me without giving anything in return.

My husband reminds me that what he needs most isn't something I can buy—it's for me to show up with love, for him and for myself. He asks me to be kind. You might wonder why he asks for something seemingly simple. But the truth is, when I'm injured or sick, being kind and showing up with love isn't easy for me. It's actually one of the hardest things. It would be much easier for me to buy a solution, hire a cleaner or cook, to lighten his load. Taking action, solving problems, is my natural go-to response, but sitting with the discomfort, staying soft and present through the tough times, that's the real work. Showing up with love and kindness is incredibly challenging for me when I'm sick or injured, but I'm willing to put in the effort because I know that when I do, it lightens the load for all of us. There are moments when I'm able to respond with care and thoughtfulness, but often I have to pause and choose my words intentionally. And sometimes I slip. I say something I don't mean or speak too quickly. In those moments I've learned to say, "I'm sorry, let me try again." When I respond with kindness in hard situations, things tend to soften. The tension eases, the conversation shifts, and it becomes a little easier to manage the situation.

Overall in our relationship, we've figured out a beautiful way to balance and share the load of life. He takes on the physical tasks of life, and I take on the mental tasks. His tasks are cleaning and maintaining all things involving the home and yard, chasing and cleaning up after our son, taking care of the dogs, long-distance driving, doing the manual labor tasks that pop up in the home. My tasks are making sure everyone's appointments are made and not forgotten, bills and taxes are dealt with, trips and activities are planned, groceries are ordered, and meals are planned and prepped, and I'm the emotional space holder for my family. We adapt as needed, depending on what kind of day I'm having. On some days I can chip in more with the household labor. As my son has gotten older and more self-sufficient, I can care for him on my own for longer stretches without straining my leg. As a family, we communicate and collaborate often so that we stay connected and maintain a healthy relationship. I would be remiss if I didn't give credit to our parents here too. Both our sets of parents help us out tremendously by watching our son while we're at work and giving us Sunday afternoons off. The old adage is true—it truly takes a village.

My husband and I have been together since I was eighteen years old. He has seen me change immensely and has been my cheerleader throughout my healing journey. He encourages me and gives me room to grow to become the person I want to be. The life I have now wouldn't be possible without him. But I also believe that a partnership doesn't have to be a marriage or a romantic relationship. A true partnership can come from anyone—a parent, a sibling, or a friend, someone who lifts you up, believes in you, is willing to tell you hard truths, and walks beside you. My hope is that people find their person or persons in this world who can show up for them unconditionally and help them in their times of need.

Fieldwork Reflection: How does being in the care-recipient or caregiver role affect you? What tough lessons have you learned in your relationship? Reflect on love: What does love mean to you, and how do you want to give or receive love?

FIELDWORK REFLECTIONS	DATE

INSIGHTS	NOTES

NEXT STEPS

FIELDWORK REFLECTIONS	DATE

ADDITIONAL NOTES

FIELDWORK REFLECTIONS	DATE

ADDITIONAL NOTES
115

FIELDWORK REFLECTIONS	DATE

ADDITIONAL NOTES

Part V:
Those Who Walk Beside Me

The company you keep

RELATIONS

Alone we can do so little; together we can do so much.

—Helen Keller

The company I keep has changed drastically over the years. Since becoming a mother, I find myself gravitating toward a small, tight-knit community built on deep, meaningful relationships. I learned that having a large circle of friends with constant group chats, social events, and check-ins makes me anxious. When I reflected on that anxiety, I discovered that it stems from a deep desire to invest energy, attention, and care in people. If I can't do that for everyone in my friend group, I feel like I'm failing them and myself. It's in my nature to have a few deeply rooted relationships rather than a wide pool of connections.

To stay true to myself and honor my values, I had to reflect carefully on which friendships I could continue to nurture and which ones were no longer sustainable. I thought about the friendships that left me feeling pressured or overwhelmed, the ones where I felt I had to respond constantly or always be available to hang out. I love those friends dearly, but I couldn't handle the self-imposed pressure anymore. I needed friendships where I felt okay not responding all the time, not hanging out often, not feeling like I was drowning in unread messages. I needed an understanding that sometimes the most I could give was a heart emoji. I had shifted my boundaries and lowered my capacity to devote time to friends, which resulted in needing to have difficult conversations to let my friends know about this shift, hoping they would understand.

I shifted and now devote most of my emotional, physical, and mental energy to raising my son, a choice I made with my whole heart. He is my greatest priority, and it's one of my deepest joys to help him develop into a kind and thoughtful human being. Because I have chosen to give him the best of me, I no longer have the capacity to sustain every relationship the way I once did. I had to make the hard decision to let some friendships go.

In the past I did not know how to handle friendship breakups well. I often found myself ghosting—pulling away without clear communication, hoping the hints were enough. I didn't have cruel intentions; I simply didn't have the tools needed to end the relationship more gracefully. I didn't know how to have those honest conversations without feeling crushing guilt or facing the fear of confrontation. Fortunately, I learned how to do so from Ozan Varol's powerful newsletter topic "Please Stop Ghosting People" and Brene Brown's lesson "Clear Is Kind. Unclear Is Unkind." They taught me that my silence and avoidance weren't protecting anyone but were actually hurting both of us. I had to be brave. I had to be willing to have uncomfortable conversations, even though they gave me sweaty hands, analysis paralysis, and a racing heart. I wrote drafts and overthought every word, and when I finally sent the message, I wanted to run away and hide from the response. Shockingly, most people responded well, with grace and understanding. There was sadness but also kindness. They sent their love and wished me well. I'm grateful for their kindness and will always hold them close in my heart.

I have also been on the receiving end of friendship breakups. Sometimes people gave me a reason; other times they simply pulled away. My heart, deeply invested in these relationships, often didn't want to let go. I felt confused, wondering what I did wrong or what changed. Over time I have learned how to approach these situations. I now become curious, try to not take it personally, and ask questions. Even though it is uncomfortable, it's worth it to see if something can be repaired in the relationship. I ask, "Hey, what's going on? I noticed a shift . . ." or "Do you still want to be friends? Because I'm feeling some distance because . . ." At times I have received vague reassurances like "Everything is fine," but nothing changed. I often found myself chasing the relationship. I put in all the work and sent check-in text messages, reaching out to see if they wanted to hang out.

Eventually I had to stop. Friendships aren't meant to be one-sided. In the end I was only hurting myself. Those breakups left their mark. I felt the pain in my heart, the sinking heaviness in my gut. I had to process the grief of losing those relationships, especially the ones tied to deep, special memories. I had to remind myself, *Let the friendship go and respect their decision.* A mantra that helps me is "I love you and I release you." I sit with the discomfort. Journal my thoughts. I send quiet, loving wishes into the universe for them, without needing a reply. I have come to accept that closure doesn't always happen in the way we imagine, but sometimes we can give it to ourselves.

As I get older, maintaining and making new friendships seems harder. People's schedules are hectic. Priorities shift. Physical limitations, like mine, create different realities. I only have so much energy, and what I can give depends on how my body feels. I can no longer meet friends for long, active afternoons or keep up with fast-paced social plans. The friends I have now understand my boundaries and needs because I've clearly communicated them. They respect my need for social breaks. They're flexible and creative about how we spend time together. They honor both who I am and what I'm capable of. Those friendships mean a lot to me; they've carried me through more than I can say.

Alongside my cherished friendships, I've also built a community of healers: therapists (massage, physical, and mental health), life coaches, acupuncturists, chiropractors, personal trainers, and a prayer group. They walk with me and support me through the varying seasons of my life. They remember the fine details of my life, follow up with genuine care, and treat me as more than just a client. At first, I was surprised by those small but thoughtful moments of being seen and remembered. Over time, they showed me what it feels like to be truly cared for within the health-care and wellness field. Their support has become essential, helping me both physically and emotionally, and they have become a meaningful part of my life.

Lastly, my family is the largest part of my community, and not just my immediate family but also my extended family. In this life I have been gifted with numerous aunts, uncles, and cousins as well as my in-laws. They are always in my corner, supporting me, cheering me on; without hesitation they are always there for me. They are my rock in turbulent times. I may not always get to see them, but I can feel their love from miles away. Their support has allowed me to take the time to heal and find not only my way back to myself but also my favorite version of myself.

During this lifetime I've learned that relationships are vulnerable, whether with family, friends, or even passing acquaintances. I'm part of the equation in these relationships—my actions, my expectations, my words all shape the dynamic. During a recent reflection I uncovered a truth about myself that was hard to admit: I often expect something in return when I give. Especially when I'm kind, open, or thoughtful, I expect that same kindness and love to be mirrored back. And when it isn't, it hurts. Kindness, I've realized, is vulnerable for me. When it's not reciprocated, I tend to take it personally. However, I experience only a handful of moments in someone's life. I don't know someone's whole life or what they're experiencing that day. Having a preset expectation of how someone should act sets me up for an opportunity to be disappointed, whereas hoping for the best and being mindful of what I do have control over, like my own thoughts, helps. People are people. They have their moments, their days. Sometimes people aren't ready to receive or don't have the capacity to reciprocate, and I'm learning how to be okay with that.

Reading *Power Moves: Ignite Your Confidence and Become a Force* by Sarah Jakes Roberts caused a perspective shift. She asked a question that stopped me in my tracks. I'm paraphrasing here, but the essence of it is "What resources or gifts can you give without expecting anything in return?" Not even acknowledgement. Not even a thank-you. That question forced me to sit with the reality that I was giving a lot to people—in terms of emotions and energy—and when I didn't receive appreciation or a similar effort in return, it left me feeling unseen or depleted.

Now I'm learning to be more intentional with my energy. I am practicing asking myself, "Am I offering this kindness freely, or am I hoping for something in return?" or "Can I give this gift without needing it to be received a certain way?" If the answer is no, I need to step back and be mindful in how I plan to show up. I no longer want to overextend my gifts, bend over backward, or become everyone's go-to person at the cost of my own peace. I don't need to be the shoulder to lean on for every person I know. I don't need to be everybody's favorite. I'm discerning. I'm more than willing to give deeply; to show up fully; to pour out my love, time, and energy, when it's a relationship built on mutual trust and respect.

I no longer offer those deeper parts of myself to everyone by default. My love is still generous, but I have grounded myself with boundaries.

It's important for me to honor my values. I want to offer kindness and compassion freely, without attaching expectations. I've learned that not every connection needs to be deep, long-lasting, or reciprocal. Sometimes I can show up with kindness, be cordial, and move on. And that's enough. That's healthy. That's growth.

Fieldwork Reflection: Reflect on your community. Who energizes you? Who drains you? What patterns do you notice? What role do you play in your relationships? What type of community do you want moving forward? What steps can you take to create it?

FIELDWORK REFLECTIONS	DATE

INSIGHTS	NOTES

NEXT STEPS

FIELDWORK REFLECTIONS	DATE

ADDITIONAL NOTES

FIELDWORK REFLECTIONS	DATE

ADDITIONAL NOTES

FIELDWORK REFLECTIONS	DATE

ADDITIONAL NOTES

PROFESSIONAL CAREER

It does not matter how slowly you go as long as you do not stop.

—Confucius

After high school I received more college rejection letters than I could count. I had to read letter after letter stating that I hadn't been accepted to attend college. I was distraught, and I sobbed. I wasn't qualified enough; my grades and test scores weren't good enough. I had just fought for my life, undergone treatment for cancer, and learned how to walk again. All I wanted was to get back to a "normal" life. I wanted to go to college and pursue a career in helping other children with cancer.

I faced a huge roadblock to achieving my goals. I had temporarily stopped going to my high school when I got sick. I was set to be a junior that year, but I needed to have chemotherapy and surgery to save my life. I was unenrolled from my high school, and my parents enrolled me in a local public school that provided homeschooling. On the days when I wasn't horribly sick from the chemo, teachers came to my home and taught me. I had homework assignments and projects to complete. My motivation to stay on top of schoolwork was simple: I didn't want to fall behind or delay graduation. Even after successfully completing my junior year from home, I felt behind and out of the loop. I transferred back to my original high school for senior year, but despite being back and recovering from all my treatments, I struggled academically. I failed miserably on the SATs. Despite the failure on the test, I persisted and completed the required courses, and I managed to graduate with my class.

Graduating from high school did not mean automatic acceptance into a college. The path ahead wasn't going to be easy, but I was not going to stop trying. I loved learning; I loved being at school. I knew I was meant to be there. I had to make a plan, find another way to get into college. I decided I would have to start from scratch and rebuild my academic foundation. I enrolled in the local community college and took numerous remedial courses and attended tutoring. After two years of building up my knowledge and achieving a 4.0 GPA, I faced my fears and applied to a university again. I decided I would apply to only one this time; I knew I couldn't face a plethora of rejection letters. After researching, making a pros-and-cons list, and considering price, I applied to the University of Texas at Austin. Several weeks later my mom called and said there was a letter from UT Austin in the mail for me. I nervously told her to open it and read it to me since I wasn't home yet. My mom read the letter out loud, and her voice went up, and then she screamed. I got in. I was accepted. My legs shook and I couldn't stand anymore. I crumpled to the floor and cried tears of joy and disbelief. I did it. I made it.

Achieving a GPA of 4.0 in community college significantly boosted my confidence, yet I was quickly humbled when I transferred to UT Austin. The courses were grueling and academically intense. I found myself struggling just to get a C in some of them. The challenge wasn't just mental; it was physical too. My classes were scattered across UT's massive campus, and there were days when my leg would give out as I climbed the stairs or steep hills. On top of that, I felt incredibly lonely. It was challenging to make friends when entering a big university two years later than most of my peers. Still, I didn't waver. I was determined to succeed.

I went to professors' and teaching assistants' office hours for extra support, leaned on tutoring services, and spent long hours in the library. Outside of academics, I reconnected with a kindhearted former high school classmate who became my roommate. Around the same time, I picked up a part-time job at J. Crew, which gave me a sense of balance and connection outside of school. There, I made friends who became some of the most amazing people I'd ever had in my life. They were adventurous, hilarious, and loving and knew how to have fun. I often sacrificed sleep to spend time with them, since I spent most of my time studying. It was worth every bit of exhaustion.

I graduated with an undergraduate degree in 2013. I made a decision I now regret, but it became a lesson that has stayed with me. I declined to walk the stage at the University of Texas at Austin. I was worried that the wait for my name to be called would take too long and my leg would lock up, inhibiting me from getting up on the stage. My parents were saddened by my decision, but they respected my choice. At that age I was too proud to ask for help and too self-conscious to risk stumbling in front of a crowd. I was also embarrassed. I didn't really know anyone at the school on a deep level. The idea of standing in front of a sea of strangers felt uncomfortable, not celebratory. That is where I was wrong—as long as my parents were there, that's what would matter. I worked hard and dedicated countless hours to studying to graduate. Most of all I should have walked for myself, regardless of no one knowing me.

Crossing the stage meant more than just graduating: It was a milestone for me. I survived my hardships and setbacks, and I continued to walk. However, I couldn't see it at that age. I hadn't done the work to heal and process my shame, anxiety, and self-consciousness. What I did have the capacity to do as a means of celebrating and honoring my accomplishment was order the cap and gown and ask a good friend to take pictures of me around campus. We had a wonderful time during the photoshoot, and those are some of my favorite pictures to this day.

The lesson I learned from the experience is to set aside my self-consciousness and worries, to show up for myself with pride. I also remind myself to give myself grace and that it's okay to celebrate differently than others. The way I show up in life is going to be different because of my experiences and circumstances.

After graduating, I enrolled in the University of Texas at San Antonio to pursue a master's degree in clinical mental health counseling. I chose that degree path to support my goal of becoming a counselor for children facing serious illnesses. I had zero hesitation about continuing school. I have always loved school. Yes, since middle school I've been that person who would be sad if I was sick and had to miss school. From school supplies to learning new topics to challenging my skills, the experience brings me joy. But not tests with highly weighted scores—that took my anxiety to another level.

By the time I was midway through my undergraduate degree, I finally learned how to manage my test anxiety. I would tell myself the day before the test that at that point I either knew the material or didn't. I had to have confidence in myself and trust that I prepared the best I could. This involved attending each class, taking good notes, making colorful study guides, and reviewing material most nights. I avoided cramming and all-nighters. Those never bode well for me. Having a full, solid seven hours of sleep and a healthy breakfast was more important for me. I had learned that being excessively worried wouldn't improve my chances of passing a test.

I completed my master's degree with honors, but I struggled with my formal education ending. I didn't know what to do with my new free time. I was used to it being consumed by classes, assignments, and studying. I had to work through that challenge and sit in the discomfort of not having a task to do and being okay with resting.

Soon after graduating I began an internship at an end-of-life care home and a children's bereavement center. To this day, sitting and being present with people in their final moments or helping their family members with grief remains some of the most meaningful work I've ever done. I was surrounded by some of the most compassionate humans I've ever met. They taught me how to hold space for others. But as fulfilling as that work was, it didn't support me financially. I decided to continue my internship at a general counseling practice to gain broader experience and support myself financially.

After a couple of years in the field, I came to a hard but honest realization: Traditional counseling wasn't the right fit for me. While I cared deeply about helping people, something inside me knew I wasn't on the right path. I was becoming burnt out emotionally. I was giving too much of myself to the work. I was struggling to balance my part-time jobs and the internship, and I was letting go of other goals in life. I knew this wasn't sustainable for me. My gut was telling me this wasn't my path anymore. I knew I was meant to serve others, but not in the way I had originally imagined.

After some deep reflection, praying, and listening to my gut, I made a tough decision: I turned in my internship license and gave myself permission to explore a new path. While I wasn't sure exactly where I was going, I trusted that by following my instincts, the right direction would reveal itself. People were shocked by this decision and said I was making a mistake. As someone who seeks reassurance from others, this made the situation challenging, but I knew I couldn't go against myself. I knew deep down that this was the right decision for me. I believe it's okay to change your goals in life. Sometimes you realize midway that a path isn't the one meant for you. I also knew that the skills I had gained and the lessons I had learned from my previous experiences weren't lost; they were transferrable and would stay with me for the rest of my life.

Drawing on experience is exactly what I did. I turned my part-time corporate job into a full-time role. To my surprise, many of the skills I learned in counseling—active listening, empathy, and emotional regulation—have translated into my current role as a quality assurance advisor. These skills have helped me navigate tough conversations, build trust with my team, and support customers in meaningful ways. While it doesn't offer the same deep fulfillment I felt working in end-of-life care and grief work, it provides me with something I deeply value: an incredible work-life balance. This job gives me the space to prioritize my health and my family. It seldom causes me stress or anxiety, offers flexibility to go to doctors' appointments, and allows me to work from home when I'm experiencing pain in my leg. In my world, having a job that supports your life in that way is a true gift. Life doesn't always take you where you thought you'd go, but I've learned to trust the process. It may not have been part of my original plan, but I know this is exactly where I'm meant to be in this season of my life.

Fieldwork Reflection: When have you experienced an unexpected change in direction? How did you cope with that? If you don't feel like you're on the right path now, how would you want to show up and manage ambiguity?

FIELDWORK REFLECTIONS	DATE

INSIGHTS	NOTES

NEXT STEPS

FIELDWORK REFLECTIONS	DATE

ADDITIONAL NOTES

FIELDWORK REFLECTIONS	DATE

ADDITIONAL NOTES

FIELDWORK REFLECTIONS	DATE

ADDITIONAL NOTES

Part VI:
What Still Stands

Lessons learned on the road,
releasing the old, and finding a new way

TEACHERS

You never know when you're creating a spark that will last forever.

—*Frank Sonnenberg*

I've learned many invaluable lessons in my life, many from teachers I've met along the way. Some of the lessons are hard to put into words, mostly because I feel them in my heart and not my head. I've picked three that have spanned my life. Each has shaped me and influenced the way I navigate through the world. One I learned before my cancer diagnosis, and it helped me persevere through hurdles in life. The second I learned just after I finished my final rounds of chemo and had recovered from surgery. The third I learned during graduate school while I was volunteering with people who were at the end of their lives.

In high school, I learned the value of do it while you can. You never know when it might be your last chance. Before my cancer diagnosis I had a truly one-of-a-kind, inspirational track and cross-country coach. He wasn't focused solely on our performance. He believed in us, invested time in us, and always encouraged us to do our best. During practice and meets he often said, "Run like it's the last race you'll ever run." I took his words to heart. At each opportunity I had to run, I gave my best, putting in my whole heart, pushing my body a little more each time. I am eternally grateful for his words of wisdom because I did indeed run my last race in 2007 and cherished every second of it. I was so present and grounded in that race that I can vividly recall the feeling of running and hearing my teammates cheering me on. In that race I beat my personal record and took home a medal.

Even though I can no longer run, I carry his words in my heart because this wisdom can be applied to so much more than just sports. Because of lessons I learned and strengths I built from participating in sports, my mental resilience was and is unwavering, so much so that it supported me in surviving my cancer journey. Just when I thought I couldn't take anymore treatments, I reminded myself of how in races, when I thought I had no more to give, I was able to push through and finish strong. That's exactly what I did. I surprised myself and kept going. Not finishing wasn't an option. Now, in my thirties, I use this lesson to do what I love, try things that scare me, and tell people how much I love them each day because I never know when it's going to be the last time.

After recovering from chemo and surgery, I was ready to learn how to drive. My parents signed me up for driving school because learning with them had been too stressful for all of us. What I didn't realize was that I was also signing up to rebuild my self-confidence. During this time I had awkwardly growing hair from being recently bald. Picture a fuzzy vulture head. I wrapped myself up in a safe cocoon of scarves and hats. I was sitting in the classroom with my colorful, flamboyant trucker hat when the instructor called me out with a booming voice: "Ma'am, do you have no manners? Don't you know it's disrespectful to wear a hat in a classroom? Remove your hat." Immediately my face reddened and became hot. Being a rule-following introvert who hates confrontation, I wanted to jump out of my body. Everyone in the classroom turned around and stared. My eyes started to swell; I didn't want to cry in front of everyone. My arm shook as I lifted it to remove my hat. I slowly removed my hat, revealing my patchy-haired head. I stared straight ahead, refusing to make eye contact with anyone.

I remained quiet for the remainder of the class. I was mortified. The little self-confidence I had was stripped away when I removed my hat. Once class was over I walked briskly out of the classroom and went straight to my mom's car. I burst into tears the second I got into the car. I told her what happened. My five-foot-two-inch-tall mother immediately got out of the car, slammed the door, and marched right up to the incredibly buff six-foot-five-inch-tall ex-military man and gave him a mouthful. He simply responded, "Ma'am, I am treating her like I would treat anyone else. She doesn't get special treatment in my class."

I overheard this and got out of the car, wiping my tears. I turned to my mother and agreed with him: "He's right, I don't want special treatment. It's okay, I can go without my hat." In that difficult moment, my driving instructor's request to remove my hat made me take my first steps on my long journey of loving myself unconditionally, building self-confidence, and not being ashamed of how I looked. I slowly started to wear my hats and scarves less and embraced my new look. By the end of driving school, I grew close to my instructor, and we always laughed. I am thankful for the lesson even though it was one of the most uncomfortable and humiliating moments in my life. I learned how to embrace new identities and step into them even if not with grace.

I now have a knack for signing myself up for uncomfortable things. In 2018 a TA from one of my graduate classes encouraged me to do an internship at an end-of-life care home. I sat with the guests who were near the end of their life, offering presence and comfort in their final moments. On more than one occasion I witnessed someone take their last breath, which is a profound honor. I wish I had written down all the lessons I learned from that time, but one lesson that stands out is how quickly and deeply you can love someone when they are honest, open, and vulnerable with you. The people I worked with were their authentic selves—no embarrassment, no hiding, no pretense. They would tell me their deepest fears, share stories they hadn't shared with anyone else, and recount their life to me, sharing their regrets and happy moments. I made it a safe space for them by not passing judgment, being present, and fully listening with my heart. This made it comfortable for them to show up as their whole self, even when their mood was sour, when they experienced pain or received bad news, when they were saddened by reflecting on their last moments on earth, when they were elated, when we told jokes, or when I baked a favorite treat of theirs. This made it easier for me to show up as my full self too.

Maybe that's something that happens when people know they're at the end of their lives. This type of love asks for nothing in return. It's the kind of love where you sit beside someone and simply bear witness to their life without judgment. I was there to help them eat, drink, and even go to the restroom. You hold space for their stories, their fears, and their silence. And when they're scared of what lies beyond, you hold their hand and stay. This skill to sit and be calm with someone at the end of their life was enhanced by an extraordinary mentor, who reminded me to breathe in deeply before entering the room, tuck in my wings, and be present. Tucking in your wings is the practice of turning down your bright, beautiful, exuberant energy and then letting in the calm, tranquil, steady energy.

This experience, and much of what I've been through in life, has made me not fear death but value life even more. What I do fear is not being able to live and experience life. To be confined to a hospital room or my home, unable to be out in the world, connecting with people, living in the moment. Not just passing through the world—that's what unsettles me. The irony is I am known for being a homebody. But there's a difference between choosing to rest at home and being forced to stay there. I truly love my alone time in the peaceful space I've created at home. It's where I rest, recharge, and reflect after spending energy out in the world. Through these moments of stillness, I've spent a lot of time reflecting on both death and love. I've come to believe that love exists in many forms: quiet and loud, fleeting and lasting. But to truly experience it, you have to live. You have to allow yourself to step into life before it ends. Challenge yourself to get uncomfortable and try something new. You never know who you'll meet or what you'll learn.

Fieldwork Reflection: Sometimes lessons we encounter in life are ones we don't want to hear or aren't ready to hear. They can be painful or humiliating, yet they remind us to keep showing up for ourselves. Over time, those same lessons can shift in meaning, depending on how we choose to see them.

What are some of the most impactful lessons you've learned in your life? How do those lessons continue to guide the way you live your life?

When was the last time you gave yourself credit for showing up, even if it wasn't perfect? How did that shift how you saw yourself?

FIELDWORK REFLECTIONS	DATE

INSIGHTS	NOTES

NEXT STEPS

FIELDWORK REFLECTIONS	DATE

ADDITIONAL NOTES
149

FIELDWORK REFLECTIONS	DATE

ADDITIONAL NOTES

FIELDWORK REFLECTIONS	DATE

ADDITIONAL NOTES

Limiting Beliefs

Most of the obstacles you face are not from the outside world but from within your own mind.

—Unknown

My healing journey deepened and became more uncomfortable the moment I stumbled across the concept of *limiting beliefs*. I had to sit with it. Something about it hit a nerve. I knew right then that this was the next layer of work I needed to do. If you're curious about what limiting beliefs are and how to begin unlearning them, I recommend Vex King's *Healing Is the New High*. In short, a limiting belief is a story you've accepted as an absolute truth you hold, one that holds you back. It took me a few days of honest reflection to uncover my own. And even then, writing them down was hard, because once they were on paper, I couldn't ignore them. I had to face them and start challenging them.

Let me walk you through one of my limiting beliefs as an example: "My body is weak and frail. Any pain I feel is a threat to me." Logically, I knew this was not true. I had endured so much in my life and survived: illnesses, treatments, surgeries, and setbacks. My body had carried me through every single one of those moments. But this belief wasn't about logic. It lived deeper, buried under fear, trauma, and old conditioning that was deep in my bones. I internalized this belief that my body was fragile and that any sign of pain meant danger. It influenced how I navigated the world—I was hyperaware, cautious, and bracing myself for the worst. My relationship with pain became complicated. To this day it is challenging for me to answer the pain-scale question of "On a scale of one to ten, how would you rate your pain?" I find myself at a loss for words. It's hard to put pain on that type of scale when you're used to pain and your baseline frequently shifts. I usually say, "Well, I wouldn't call it pain. It annoys me and causes discomfort, but it's not painful." I usually get a blank stare from my doctors with that type of answer.

My tolerance and the way I handle pain is inconsistent; it's situational. My pain tolerance after surgeries is quite high. A true "ten" pain for me is when it's soul-crushing, numbing pain after a surgery. When bones are removed and replaced with titanium and then being asked to get up and walk around the next day. Oddly, I can handle the "ten" pain because I know it's temporary; I know it will get better. Typically, the day after a surgery, I'm off the opioid medication because I would rather manage the pain myself than deal with a groggy mind and other undesirable side effects. I take a small dose of acetaminophen or NSAIDs as needed. Whereas when I experience a minor pain, my mind and body spiral, which exacerbates the pain.

Physically, I would rate minor pain as a three or a four, but the issue is what this pain does to my mental state. My mental state internalizes this pain as a ten. My thoughts will race as I try to recollect if anything I did caused the pain. I believe I do this because I'm terrified that it's time for me to replace my leg or that my body is developing a new health condition. I spiral thinking about what options I'll have for surgery, how much time I'll have to take off, what help I need to get, how it will affect my family, the recovery time, and so on. To stop myself from spiraling I tell myself, "You are time traveling." It's my reminder to come back to the present. I ground myself by noticing where I am and what I see, hear, smell, and feel. Then I sit with my pain. I acknowledge it, accept it for what it is, and then release it from my mind.

After years of therapy and self-help practices, I had a breakthrough in May 2025. For the first time I fully allowed myself to feel my pain. To sit in the discomfort of it. I didn't resist it. I located it in my body, listened to it, and noticed how it moved and shifted the longer I sat with it. I didn't judge it or myself, or wish it away, or try to make it something else. I let it be exactly what it was. Most importantly, I didn't panic. I didn't spiral. After sitting with my pain, I got up slowly and tended to my aching leg. I am incredibly proud of that moment. It was the result of years of work—practicing in therapy and learning how to sit with all kinds of pain, both emotional and physical. My pain didn't become suffering, because I gave it space. I honored its presence. Pain is part of life. You can't avoid it. But you can decide how to relate to it. You can prolong it by wishing it away, pretending it's not there, or dwelling on it. Or you can choose to learn how to cope, to sit with it, to care for yourself through it. I am still learning, still practicing, but I've come a long way.

The way I move through the pain now is nothing like how I used to.

Lately, as I reflect more deeply, I've started to uncover the beliefs that shaped how I once responded to pain. One of the most persistent is that there should be a limit to how much pain one person has to endure in a lifetime. That belief lived in my unconscious mind for years. It influenced how I coped, how I fought, and how I grieved. I decided to dig deeper to see if there was more underneath it. I learned that I held the core belief that all things are limited and scarce. I believed good health was finite, that there was a limit to how many times I could ask for help—from friends, from family. I was afraid that needing too much would push people away, that I'd become a burden, that the people I loved would quietly start to distance themselves. I believed there was a limit to how many times I could fall ill or how much pain I could endure before I broke. I believed time was scarce, that everything needed to be done right away or it wouldn't happen at all. Beneath that belief was fear, that I might run out of time for what I love, especially the moments with my son.

These limiting beliefs ran silently in the background, steering my life with fear and anguish, but they weren't true. The truth is my loved ones don't keep the score. They show up without question, just as I do for them. Pain has never broken me; I have always gotten back up, even if slowly. Time feels scarce when I rush, but I lose more of it when I'm not present, when I dwell on the past or try to control the future. Going slow is the fastest way forward. We don't know how much time we'll have, so spend it doing the things you love with the people you love. When it comes to material things and a scarcity mindset, I remind myself that I cannot take any of it with me when I take my final step, my final breath, on this earth.

These shifts help me rewrite the stories I tell myself. My life is full of experiences that disprove these limiting beliefs. I'm learning that not all limits are bad—some are healthy. They help me honor my values and create space for what really matters. The problem arises when limits form unconsciously and begin to influence our lives without us realizing it. I've learned to notice these hidden limits. They reveal themselves through guilt, shame, discomfort, and anguish. Those feelings are signals, reminders to pause and reflect on my thoughts. I take time to sort through what is really underneath the situation and ask myself, "Is there a belief driving this? And is it still one I want to continue?" This takes work and time; it is tiring, I know. However, in my world it's worth putting in the work, because the reward of living a life aligned with your values and beliefs, with less stress, is fulfilling. I'm learning how to slow down, act with intention, and create a life that mirrors the person I aspire to be. In that, I find balance and security. I stay mindful of my thoughts, and when one throws me off balance, I ask myself, "Is this a limiting belief? Is this rooted in fear? Is this belief helping me or hurting me?"

There are layers in the healing process, and each layer unfolds when you're ready to face and process it. Go slow and be kind to yourself while processing each layer. I believe that when you free yourself from your limiting beliefs and create new, empowering ones, you are one step closer to the person you were always meant to be.

Fieldwork Reflection: What might your life look like if you wrote new beliefs for yourself? What sorts of limiting beliefs have held you back in your life? How did you overcome them?

FIELDWORK REFLECTIONS	DATE

INSIGHTS	NOTES

NEXT STEPS

FIELDWORK REFLECTIONS	DATE

ADDITIONAL NOTES

FIELDWORK REFLECTIONS	DATE

ADDITIONAL NOTES

FIELDWORK REFLECTIONS	DATE

ADDITIONAL NOTES

PHILOSOPHY SWITCH

Change your thoughts and you change your world.

—Norman Vincent Peale

No pain, no gain is a philosophy I held on to since I was a young child. I would white-knuckle through pain and keep going. I was raised not to cry when I got hurt and to never complain about pain. If you could do so, you were held in high regard, as it was proof that you were strong and courageous. This philosophy helped me survive and endure some of the most excruciating pain I experienced in my life. I became so good at it that I disconnected from my body and learned to put on a front when I was in pain. This mindset came with repercussions because I applied it across the board.

After a decade of this mindset, I discovered I had trouble moving parts of my body. I realized this when my husband and I were working out together. He instructed me to flex one of my muscles, and as hard as I tried, I couldn't connect my mind to my muscle to get it to flex. I then tested other areas of my body, and sure enough, there were multiple muscles I couldn't activate on command. This was concerning, but I didn't know what I could do about it. I carried on with life and my philosophy of no pain, no gain. Even though I didn't express my pain externally, internally I would shake. My core trembled, my gut tightened, and my head flooded with panicked thoughts. On the outside, I appeared calm and still, but inside, I was falling apart. I believe this occurred because I suppressed the external expression of pain, so it manifested internally and became trapped. I felt distressed by the symptoms. I knew I had to unlearn this coping technique of disassociating from my body to avoid feeling pain. I had to figure out how to process my fear of pain: to feel it, give it space, and then release it.

After my knee-revision surgery I went to physical therapy. During physical therapy the therapist had to break up scar tissue and manually stretch my leg. This was not a pleasant experience and would send electric shocks to my brain. The physical therapist asked whether the therapy was too intense for me, and I would always answer, "No, I can handle this." I ignored the shrill internal cries from my body begging for the therapist to stop. I would just focus on my breath, disassociate from the pain, and let the therapist continue their work. This practice became problematic because it resulted in injuries for me. I didn't tell the therapist to stop when the pain was too much. The therapist had no clue they were pushing my body too hard. I consulted with my acupuncturist about the pain I was experiencing during and after physical therapy. In response she referred me to a new massage therapist, who specialized in pain resolution and soft tissue.

At the first visit the massage therapist asked questions about why I was there to see her. I told her about my history and the struggle I was currently having with my body and my response to handling and managing pain. After I told her my story, she shared something that stayed with me: "The greatest power, the greatest strength, comes from the gentlest touch." She began massaging the scar tissue and other sensitive areas around my leg with a gentle but firm touch. It wasn't painful; I didn't have to grin and bear it. Most shockingly, the gentle approach was effective. My body responded to the gentle, calming touch and relaxed. My leg became more flexible, and the scar tissue wasn't as sensitive. My massage therapist smiled and shared that the healing process doesn't have to be painful.

To this day, I still see her, and through our many sessions together she has helped me not only with my pain but also with my mind and muscle connection. The slow, gentle massages, stretches, and exercises she taught me have helped me reactivate muscles I hadn't been able to control on command. I continue the journey of retraining and strengthening my muscles with a personal trainer twice a month. These practices have allowed me to move more easily through the world with less discomfort and pain. Overall, I learned there is a time and place for white-knuckling through pain. It's useful in emergencies, but it shouldn't be an everyday, all-purpose tool. In daily life, it's okay to speak up when something hurts and ask about alternative healing options.

It took me a while to learn that showing pain isn't a sign of weakness. This lesson truly sank in after I witnessed a family member suffering. I told them, "You don't have to put up a front. You don't have to hide your pain and pretend everything is fine. We are family, and family is here for you. It's okay to tell us when you're hurting. We want to support you in any way we can, but we can't help if we don't know you're in pain." As I spoke those words, I realized they were exactly what I had needed to hear years ago—that it's okay to tell others when you're hurting. I used to believe that suppressing pain made me stronger, but I've learned that true strength lies in acknowledging it, asking for help, and giving yourself time to heal.

By slowing down, being curious, and listening to my body, I've begun to reconnect with myself and relate to pain in a new way. Massages, somatic experiencing therapy, and intentional rest have all supported this process. And it's not just my own pain I've been learning to work with. As an empath, I used to absorb people's pain and carry it with me. However, I've come to understand that other people's pain is theirs to hold. I can sit with them and offer comfort and support them, but it's not my job to take their pain on as my own. It took me many years to learn this.

Sometimes I wonder why I didn't learn this lesson sooner in life, especially when I was working toward becoming a counselor. However, I'm learning that there is a time and place for every lesson to reveal itself. During my counseling internship, I was becoming burnt out, and my empathy was at maximum capacity. I carried all the emotions home with me. At the time, I couldn't figure out how to stop feeling and absorbing everyone else's pain. I would turn to journaling to process, but it wasn't enough. It wasn't until years later, when I went to counseling to specifically address this, that I began to understand the weight I was carrying. There, I uncovered that I felt like I owed the world because I survived cancer while many others did not. I wanted to give back what others gave to me—almost like I was indebted for all the goodness and miracles I received in life. I thought it was my duty to support other people and hold their emotions. That's when I decided to reflect more and process that I wasn't indebted for all the good things I received in life. I didn't have to pay back the world—all the good things were gifts without strings, without expectation.

Even though I decided the counseling career was not for me, I still wanted to figure out how to give thanks, to find a way to love and support people without absorbing their emotions and becoming drained. That's when I learned I could be present and hold space for someone without taking on the heaviness of the emotions. When I get overwhelmed with emotions, I take a moment to breathe slowly and intentionally and remind myself that the emotions aren't mine to hold. Sometimes I even have to step outside, reset, and breathe it all out. This new way of supporting people allows me to show up not only for others but also for myself. Learning how to handle pain and intense emotions has helped me make progress with my leg and with other challenges I face. I no longer push through pain to the point of injury or drown in other people's emotions. Instead, I'm slowing down and allowing myself to heal fully in both body and mind.

One of the more challenging parts I'm still working through is rebuilding trust—both by learning to trust my body and with my body learning to trust me. I want to believe that my body knows how to heal and that it is strong. And I want my body to trust that it's safe now and that I will advocate for it. The practices I'm integrating into my life, along with the time I'm taking to heal, are helping to build that trust. Pain still makes me anxious from time to time, but when it does, I try to meet it with grace and patience. This journey of trust and safety is ongoing, but for the first time in a long while, I feel like my body and I are on the same side.

Fieldwork Reflection: When life didn't go according to my grand plans, I had a habit of getting swept away in my emotions and dwelling on the issue, making myself feel worse. Now I approach life's surprises and pain with curiosity and seek an opportunity to learn. I pause and ask myself, "What lesson can be learned here? What skill can I practice here? Is it patience, faith, trust, courage, practicing presence, an opportunity to go slow?"

What would a philosophy switch look like for you? What's another way you can look at life?

Now, I'll be honest: There are days when I don't have the capacity to learn a lesson or when I don't feel like reflecting. In those moments I try to accept what is and not to assign judgment to the situation, and move on.

FIELDWORK REFLECTIONS	DATE

INSIGHTS	NOTES

NEXT STEPS

FIELDWORK REFLECTIONS	DATE

ADDITIONAL NOTES

FIELDWORK REFLECTIONS	DATE

ADDITIONAL NOTES

FIELDWORK REFLECTIONS	DATE

ADDITIONAL NOTES

REFLECTION

You are as old as the risks you take. In many ways, aging is not the process of growing old, but rather the slow death of becoming overly protective, scared, and worried about losing what you have. Youth is found in the energy of going for it, taking the risk, and trusting that you'll figure it out along the way.

—*James Clear*

Reflection has become an essential part of my life. It allows me to look at life from different perspectives. I love taking time to reflect, whether it's on my day, my progress, or something that intrigues me, like a quote, a book, or a podcast. Reflection gives me the chance to sit with new ideas and see them from different angles. There are times when something I read or listen to really affects me and resonates deeply. I feel a visceral response, as if I was meant to hear it in that moment, understand it, and apply it to my own life. One of those moments came when I discovered the quote included at the beginning of this chapter.

I subscribe to James Clear's *3-2-1 Thursday* newsletter, in which he provides ideas, quotes, and questions. James Clear is a writer and speaker who focuses on habits and continuous self-improvement. He is the author of *Atomic Habits*—a good read! This particular quote from his newsletter struck a chord because it speaks to something I've only recently begun to work on. Seventeen years post-cancer, I've noticed how much I've swung like a pendulum in the way I relate to my leg, between protectiveness and fear on one side and impulsiveness on the other.

When I was younger, I leaned toward the fearless end, rarely thinking through my actions, which often led to injury. For example, there was the time I chased my dog down a busy street—and another time, with a different dog, when I lunged to grab her legs before she could dash off. That decision ended with both my knees slamming into concrete. The bigger lesson here: I need to stop having dogs that run away. All jokes aside, these impulsive decisions—and many others over the years— led to injuries that put me out of commission for weeks at a time. Now, at thirty-three, if a dog escapes, I calmly say, "She will come back," and wait on my porch, sitting in my chair, trusting that she will return. For the record, she returned within minutes to resume her plush couch life. The ability to stay calm in moments of chaos is the positive side of my change. But the difficult part? It's managing and recalibrating the part of life where I have become fearful.

Just as the quote says, I've grown overly protective, scared, and worried about losing what I have. I've become so protective of my leg that it's difficult for me to let my guard down and have fun. I'm terrified of getting hurt, being out of commission for weeks, and losing my ability to explore the world, go out with family, and spend time with friends. And yet, by trying so hard to protect myself, I'm still losing. Because when fear takes over, I'm not truly living. I'm not in the moment. I'm not letting myself have fun, which keeps me from experiencing life fully. I hold myself back. The real me—the one who's goofy and spontaneous, the one who loves to dance around the house and take chances—doesn't come out as often. My trauma taught me to play it safe and protect myself. Now I'm doing the work of learning how to hold both truths: the instinct to protect myself and the deep desire to let my true free-spirit self come out. It's the part of me that's been wounded and the part that just wants to live freely. For me, it's not about being perfectly healed or always happy. It's about letting the dark and the light sides of myself coexist together, balancing them, letting my entire self exist.

Fieldwork Reflection: I invite you to reflect on this quote. If it doesn't resonate with you, that's okay. What would it look like to honor your need for protection and safety and your desire to grow? How do you work to overcome your fears?

FIELDWORK REFLECTIONS	DATE

INSIGHTS	NOTES

NEXT STEPS

FIELDWORK REFLECTIONS	DATE

ADDITIONAL NOTES

FIELDWORK REFLECTIONS	DATE

ADDITIONAL NOTES

FIELDWORK REFLECTIONS	DATE

ADDITIONAL NOTES

Part VII:
Walking Myself Home

Healing and choosing wellness

Healing

Just when the caterpillar thought the world was over, it became a butterfly.

—Unknown

I needed to heal for me, not for anyone else. I wanted to be the best version of myself, the highest version I was called to be. My true self got buried under my trauma, anxiety, fears, and depression, especially when I tried to ignore those feelings. I longed for a life where I could wake up with lightness and energy instead of dread. These constant overwhelming feelings led me to begin my healing journey. I started therapy in August 2022, and as I write this in May 2025, I've consistently been in therapy ever since.

I've worked with different therapists. I started with postpartum therapy twice a week, gradually moving to once a week, then every other week, and eventually once a month. Along the way, I worked with different therapists, each bringing their own style and approach. I changed therapists a few times, sometimes because I wanted a different therapy style or because of insurance in-network coverage availability or out-of-pocket cost, and other times because our schedules no longer aligned. However, each one helped me in a meaningful way. They normalized what I was experiencing with postpartum depression and anxiety. They educated me on what happens to the body after giving birth and the impacts of breastfeeding. That knowledge I gained and the validation I received helped me feel normal.

My last postpartum counselor recommended that I seek out someone trained in trauma, specifically to help me process my cancer journey. Until then, I had never thought of my cancer experience as trauma. When I was told I was cancer-free and my leg had healed, I hastily attempted to return to my old life as if nothing had changed. I never gave myself the space to process what had happened. I buried it. For over a decade I pushed the experience aside, until the postpartum depression and anxiety became the final straw. I couldn't keep it together anymore. My mind tried to bury the memories, refusing to revisit the experience, but my body never forgot. It carried the weight until it began to break. When I was postpartum, I started shaking during anxious moments. I would tremble and shake internally. I could feel my blood quivering in my veins, and I had little control over calming my body. I would try to ignore these sensations. I kept going on with life; I didn't want to tell people what I was experiencing.

Eventually my body made me listen: I developed a double ear infection so severe that it affected my hearing for weeks. My digestion worsened, and I was constantly getting sick. I saw specialists for these symptoms and received treatment for my ears and stomach, which helped, but I was still struggling. Deep down, I knew my body was trying to tell me something—it was stuck, holding on to something. I was fortunate that my therapist didn't focus solely on my postpartum symptoms. She looked at my whole self. With this perspective, she encouraged me to find a therapist who specialized in working with cancer survivors and advised me that I could benefit from processing what I was currently experiencing and my past experience with cancer. I didn't hesitate. I did research to seek out a specialized therapist, and once I found one I made an appointment as soon as possible.

From our first session, I knew I had found the right person. With her background of working at MD Anderson and extensive experience supporting cancer survivors, I didn't have to explain the treatments or medical jargon. She understood. There was sincerity in her presence—she was kind, authentic, and witty. For the first time ever, I felt safe enough to open up, to cry, be angry, and grieve. She held space for all of it. Through our work together, I began to acknowledge what I had been through and explored my life through different lenses. The work of revisiting my past was intense but necessary. Despite the discomfort, I could feel myself making progress. Life began to make more sense. I was shedding decades of invisible weight: fear, anxiety, and buried pain I didn't even realize I was carrying.

After months of talk therapy, I understood my thoughts and emotions better. Despite a calmer mind, my body was still tense. I would shake in response to pain or discomfort, even when I felt mentally steady. It was a contradiction I couldn't figure out how to resolve. I felt confused and defeated. No matter how grounded I felt in my thoughts, I couldn't convince my body it was safe.

That's when I realized I had disconnected from my body. I dissociated to survive the cancer treatments, surgeries, and side effects, but I never returned to my body after surviving cancer. I was still afraid. Afraid I would lose my leg, afraid to feel intense pain, afraid another illness would happen. I sat with that realization, determined to figure out what to do next. That's when I remembered learning about somatic experiencing (SE) therapy during my counseling internship. SE focuses on how trauma lives in the body by focusing on the body's sensations and nervous system reactions. I discussed this idea with my therapist, and she agreed it could be helpful. Unfortunately, she wasn't trained in SE, which made me seek out a therapist who specialized in this type of therapy. It took time to find an SE therapist who took my insurance and had availability. But I was determined, and eventually I found one.

I started attending therapy twice a week. Every other session left me emotionally drained. This was one of the most taxing therapies I had ever experienced. My therapist called what I felt afterward a therapy hangover. My husband could always tell when I had a session because of my blotchy face after crying. Reconnecting with the body I hadn't felt safe in for almost two decades meant facing long-buried emotions and past experiences, and the process was a shock to my system. Over time, though, the progress I had hoped for began to take shape in ways I didn't fully expect. I started to feel myself in my body again. At first it was subtle, like noticing the ground beneath my feet or the sound of my own breath.

I was slowly reconnecting with myself. It was a fascinating, almost surreal experience to feel myself sink back into my body. My mind and body were finally coming back into alignment. Looking back, I realize why I hadn't recognized the person in the mirror: I had been completely disconnected from myself. My reflection felt like that of a stranger, someone I was observing rather than inhabiting. But little by little, that started to change. I began to feel grounded, more present, more like me. The more I reconnected with my body, the more familiar I became to myself. I wasn't just existing; I was returning to myself. I was beginning to feel safer. It became easier to sit with the pain and cope with stress in life.

After several months of this work, I can say I am more in tune with my body. When uncomfortable sensations or emotions arise, my body guides me. It shows me what needs attention, what needs to be healed, what needs to be released, and what can be learned from it. My body "pings" or "nudges" me toward different areas, drawing my focus inward, helping me settle into those spaces and process whatever ideas or images surface. I am still in awe of how my body helps guide me through the next layer of healing. Every time I sit with my body, give it space, and offer my full attention, it reveals what needs to be processed next. An example of this is how I knew the next part of my healing journey would be diving into a different type of therapy, internal family systems (IFS). This idea came to me while listening to a guest talking about it on a podcast. At that moment a "ping" came to me, a knowing that this was my next step.

I did research on this therapy and found a therapist. Through our sessions, I've been uncovering the reasons behind my behaviors and getting to know different parts of myself on a deeper level. The therapy is teaching me to be curious about and compassionate toward myself and how to love my whole self. In the beginning it was draining for me and involved a lot of crying on my end, but with the work I have done I can feel myself becoming more familiar and aligned with my true self.

As you can tell, this healing journey is a work in progress, and I'm grateful for and proud of how far I've come. I am finally starting to truly love and accept my whole, imperfect self. I believe healing is the greatest gift you can give yourself. It's not easy or quick, but the outcome is transformative and remarkable. Find the right person or people to walk alongside you. Ask questions. Be curious. Get uncomfortable. Challenge yourself.

Fieldwork Reflection: What is preventing you from healing? What do you need to start your journey, and who can support you? What is it costing you to not heal?

FIELDWORK REFLECTIONS	DATE

INSIGHTS	NOTES

NEXT STEPS

FIELDWORK REFLECTIONS	DATE

ADDITIONAL NOTES

FIELDWORK REFLECTIONS	DATE

ADDITIONAL NOTES

FIELDWORK REFLECTIONS	DATE

ADDITIONAL NOTES

BODYWORK

*The body remembers what the mind forgets. In the
healing, we come home to it, piece by piece.*

—Unknown

For years, I hated anyone touching my leg. Over time, bodywork became one of the most important parts of my healing. Even the lightest touch would send an indescribable shock, like an alarm going off, shooting straight up to my brain. It felt like my leg was having its own version of a panic attack, afraid it might have to endure another invasive surgery or be amputated altogether. After my surgeries in 2007 and 2023, I went through months of physical therapy, relearning how to walk, balance, gain strength, and trust my leg again. I progressed from a wheelchair to a walker, then a cane, and finally to walking on my own. Physical therapy helped me regain strength and mobility but did not resolve the shock response I would experience when my leg was touched. Eventually I added massage therapy.

I've worked with various massage therapists, each offering their own specialized techniques to help my body heal. After several years of doing massages on and off, my leg started to get used to being touched, and my scar tissue was finally being broken down. My massage therapists also taught me how to massage myself when I experienced swelling or pain. It even took time for my leg to adjust to my own touch. During massage therapy, one of my therapists recommended I try acupuncture to help me learn how to relax my body overall. It took a couple of months to act on that suggestion, but I'm grateful I did. I found an incredible acupuncturist who takes care of me by using needles, cupping, and moxa. She has helped me achieve a level of relaxation and calm I hadn't been able to experience before. My body resisted at first, as it had with massage therapy. I began to realize that each new practice would bring its own period of adjustment.

Around the same time I also started seeing a chiropractor for chronic hip and back pain. Years of walking and sitting with poor alignment had taken a toll, especially with one leg being slightly shorter than the other. That imbalance had thrown my body out of sync. Fortunately, my chiropractor could order custom orthotics to correct the length difference, which helped me feel more balanced. Another chiropractor noticed something I hadn't said out loud: that I still got anxious whenever I experienced pain. He gently suggested a few books and introduced me to the practice of qigong. Qigong gave me a way to meditate while moving slowly and intentionally. It became a way to reconnect with my body though calm, rhythmic motion, without fear.

Reflecting on my journey, each of my practitioners has invested in me and made sure I have the best quality of life possible. I see my practitioners not only as healers but also as teachers. I ask questions and learn everything I can from them. They teach me how to care for my body and how to move it properly without putting unnecessary strain on my other leg. When my body and mind have received the care they need and I've learned all I can, I know it's time to move on. The experience of healing and reconnecting with my body has continuously uncovered the next natural step for me to work on. When I started working on one thing, someone would recommend that I try another practice.

People helped me see my blind spots, but I had to pause and ask myself if their suggestions truly aligned with what I needed. I have learned that no one can know me better than myself. I have an old habit of wanting to be agreeable, saying yes so others feel valued and appreciated. But I've come to understand that it's okay to politely decline or table it for another time. In learning what works for me, I have also learned what doesn't. Group workout classes, for example, aren't a good fit. I tend to get competitive, push myself too hard, and end up hurting myself. The same goes for working out with friends. For some people it's a motivator. For me, when I saw how much they achieved, I wanted to reach that level too, which just wasn't possible for me. I've learned to be my own competition.

What works best for me is going slow, being intentional, and staying connected to how my body feels. My old athlete mentality still tries to take over, especially when I'm in a gym with other people. I've learned to check in with myself, to move with care, and to stay focused on what truly supports my healing, not on the pressure to prove anything to anyone. I still slip into old habits sometimes, but now I know how to return to myself. Progress for me looks different these days. I am no longer pushing to the point of exhaustion; I'm learning to listen to my body and honor its slower pace.

This journey has taught me that healing isn't about proving anything to others. It's about being honest with and loyal to yourself. It's about letting go of what no longer serves you and recognizing what truly helps. It's also about having the courage to speak up for your needs and giving yourself permission to grow at your own pace. I don't need to prove my worth by gritting my teeth through pain and insisting I'm fine. I am learning how to trust my body and its signals, limits, and wisdom. Through these bodywork practices, I've learned how to reconnect with myself. My body is now something I live in, move through, listen to, and care for. The bodywork continues, but now it's rooted in compassion, not punishment; in curiosity, not control. I don't just feel like I'm healing—I feel like I'm finally coming back to myself.

Fieldwork Reflection: What does coming back to yourself look and feel like? How has your mindset changed over the years?

FIELDWORK REFLECTIONS	DATE

INSIGHTS	NOTES

NEXT STEPS

FIELDWORK REFLECTIONS	DATE

ADDITIONAL NOTES

FIELDWORK REFLECTIONS	DATE

ADDITIONAL NOTES

FIELDWORK REFLECTIONS	DATE

ADDITIONAL NOTES

DAILY DEVOTION

The greatest wealth is health.

—Virgil

I enjoy daydreaming. Every now and then I ponder whether I would rather win the lottery or have great health and a completely healed leg that would allow me to run and do any activity I wanted. I choose health. Money can't buy what I dream of. Coming back to reality, I like to think about what is possible: investing time, energy, and money in taking care of my health. This is what I work toward each day. I strive to be the healthiest version of myself mentally and physically. Throughout my journey I feel I have grown closer to that version.

What has helped me stay committed to my journey of healing and self-growth is a combination of discipline, motivation, and stubbornness. I've seen the difference the healing process has made in my life. It has helped me breathe easier, relax more deeply, and stay present. My motivation is layered: It's my family, my desire to explore the world, and my spiritual belief that I am here to serve others. For me to fully show up in life, to travel, to connect, to give, I have to feel well in both body and mind. To do that I had to drastically change my lifestyle. I started looking at my daily life and had to be honest with myself. What needs to change?

What practices and beliefs can help me stay grounded and be well?

One of the most important things for me is gratitude. I practice it in small ways throughout the day. Every morning when I rise from my own bed, I treasure that gift. Hugging my son, kissing my husband, or simply feeling my feet touching the ground are moments I cherish. At the end of the day, I reflect on all the good things that happened to me. Even the smallest things matter: a kind word, a good laugh, a smile from a stranger, a quiet moment. They all count.

Another major shift has been my diet. In May 2023 I was officially diagnosed with ulcerative colitis. The previous year I had been suffering and getting horribly sick within minutes of eating something that didn't agree with me. The effects of eating foods that didn't agree with me lingered for weeks. It got to the point where I was obsessively trying to figure out on my own what was causing it. I'd restrict foods and experiment with eating at different times of day. Nothing was working. I finally surrendered—I asked for a referral to a gastroenterologist and had a coloscopy. My inflammation levels were through the roof. I had bleeding and harmful bacteria in my intestine. I was also tested for allergies, and I discovered that I'm allergic to many foods I love, like oats and peanuts.

The doctor and I collaborated on a game plan. I asked questions: What are the chances I can cure this without medication? Is this caused by all the medications I've been on in the past? Can we try to heal this without medication first and, if that doesn't work, try medication? I also got a second opinion, and the doctor agreed with the findings and recommendations of the first doctor. The first step I took was working with a dietician to help me understand more about foods and which ones caused inflammation (my main source was refined carbs and sugar). I did a lot of research, educating myself on foods and how they affect the body, how certain foods can cause harm and how others can be medicine. I had to figure out what worked for my body. It took a year of figuring out the "right" foods for my body and giving in to taking a small dose of medicine to help me.

I no longer eat fast food. I keep fried foods to a minimum (yes, once in a blue moon I'll happily steal some fries from someone's plate or share an order with friends). I lean toward gluten-free options and minimal dairy and eat mostly lean meats and seafood. I don't drink alcohol—it wreaks havoc on my whole body. Low-caffeine and herbal teas are my regular go-to. I had to say goodbye to coffee because too much caffeine irritates my gut and increases my anxiety. This was upsetting for me because the smell and taste of coffee made me feel at home. The experience of having coffee reminds me of the times I spent at my grandparents' home and the family parties that ended late with coffee and pastries. Both my grandparents have been deceased for many years now, and the big family gatherings have ended, which made giving up coffee even more bitter. Pun intended.

However, I've found new ways to reminisce over my fond memories of my grandparents and to celebrate their lives. One of the ways is through cooking. I'm a self-taught cook and baker. I learned techniques and recipes by observing my grandmother while she was in the kitchen. She never wrote her recipes down. I begged her to write down her rice recipe for me. She said she would try her best since she adds dashes and pinches of things. To this day I haven't been able to make the rice exactly the same as hers. I'm convinced she left out a secret ingredient or technique to leave me guessing for the rest of my life. In addition to my observations, I learned by reading cookbooks and watching cooking shows (shout-out to Ina Garten and Alton Brown).

I cook and bake most of my meals and desserts at home, especially now, due to my stomach issues. I adapted many of my grandmother's traditional Tex-Mex and American recipes to make them lighter and easier for me to digest. I'll be honest: Not everyone is a fan of the "healthier" version of Tex-Mex food I make, but it makes me happy because I can eat it without consequences later. I'm fortunate that I love being in the kitchen, especially when it comes to baking. It's a science and an art to me. It captures my full attention to the point where there's no room for any other thoughts. I did have to relearn the rules of baking when I had to switch to gluten-free, but that was an exciting challenge for me. I desire to master the art of making something gluten-free so delicious that you wouldn't know it was missing the gluten. I admit I have failed many times in my experimental baking, but I have had some successes.

I not only had to relearn the rules of baking but also had to address the physical impact cooking and baking have on my leg. When cooking, you spend a lot of time on your feet. On the days when I am experiencing leg pain or recovering from an injury or surgery, cooking is a challenge. My leg tires quickly from standing and bending down to get different pots and appliances out. Other parts of my body try to compensate, but this results in overall fatigue. I had to adapt and figure out a different approach to cooking. For example, if I'm going to be preparing a recipe that has a lot of ingredients or steps, I break up the recipe over a span of several days. On day one I measure out the required ingredients and then stop there. Then, the following day, I chop all the produce needed. Finally, on the day that I need the meal, it's easy for me to assemble everything in a shorter amount of time. As for the recipes that require me to keep a close eye on or stand over a hot comal for a while, like when making tortillas, I bought a portable cooktop. I set it up on my kitchen table, put on some good music, sit down, and cook.

On the days when I'm experiencing a lot of pain, my husband is the cook. He's a good one! To this day we take turns cooking. If we have our hands full with life events and managing my pain is challenging, we have family members or friends come over and have a cooking party. Everybody pitches in and preps meals for us for the week and helps clean up after. These cooking parties are a lot of fun and much appreciated.

I also had to modify some of my hobbies. As a former self-proclaimed foodie, not going out to eat as often was challenging. I've always loved going to new restaurants, trying a variety of foods. That was the go-to date-night ritual for my husband and me. It's challenging to eat out at restaurants, but not impossible. I give myself time to research and find a new-to-us place that accommodates my dietary needs. I don't always have the opportunity to research the restaurant, or a friend or family member picks the place. That's when I have to remind myself to breathe and not stress and that there will be something for me. I can always ask the server to see if they can steam some vegetables for me or grill a piece of chicken.

I've learned that stress also wreaks havoc on my digestive system. My digestive system, in its own way, is teaching me to go with the flow. This way of life was a transition for me—it took multiple attempts of trying again and again. In the past I tried many times to eat well and continuously failed to commit to this lifestyle. I loved cheeseburgers and milkshakes far too much and despised the fishy taste of seafood. It took being diagnosed with ulcerative colitis to get my act together and stay committed to a healthy diet. Eventually I grew to love the new way I eat. I gush over the delicious grilled-vegetable plates and swoon over the in-season produce at restaurants. I'm that person who knows her fishmonger and gets excited to visit and purchase fresh produce at farmers' markets.

As I uncover what truly supports my body, I've begun studying Ayurveda, the traditional medicine system from India. I see this as another step in my lifelong learning. Each day offers an invitation to learn, integrate, and grow in how I care for myself. This journey of understanding what supports me is still unfolding, and I know that as time goes on my needs will shift. I will stay open to change and remind myself that it's not about achieving perfection but about remaining curious and patient with myself.

In addition to making dietary changes, I had to make a commitment to move my body. By the fifteenth year of living with my titanium leg, I learned that if I didn't move and exercise my body regularly, my muscles atrophied. When that happened, exploring new places on foot became incredibly challenging, if not impossible. Being limited to my home is not a life I want for myself, which is why I choose to wake up early and work out. Let me be clear: I'm not doing high-intensity workouts. My routines are grounded, steady, and intentional. My exercises consist of stretches, strength training with light weights and resistance bands, and slow cycling on my stationary bike.

If I fail to wake up early, I pause to check in with myself. I listen to my body to see if I need to rest or need a slower start. If I have the energy to move my body, I take a walk or work out my arms during my lunch break. And if none of that happens, I can always count on my son requesting an impromptu dance party. He loves inventing new moves and insists that we try them with him. His joy is contagious. Those moments usually leave me out of breath and laughing, reminding me that movement doesn't always have to be structured or serious. I'm grateful for him and his natural ability to make life light and more fun.

On rest days I prioritize recovery. I try to make time for the sauna, especially in the winter. The heat helps ease the aches in my body. I'm intentional about what I take on during rest days. I avoid tasks that demand too much physically, and when I really need to go slow, I turn to meditative practices.

Meditation, journaling, prayer, breathwork, and qigong have become my favorite ways to ground myself. These practices get me out of my head, reset my body, and bring me back to the present. They bring clarity to what I'm really feeling rather than letting my thoughts spiral and get tangled up in my head. Journaling especially brings me joy. I reflect on my thoughts, what I'm learning, and how I'm growing. I also love reading and listening to self-help books and podcasts and writing down the takeaways that resonate.

Getting into these practices wasn't easy. Meditation and breathwork, in particular, took a lot of trial and error. It took me a couple of years to figure out what actually worked for me, but the reward has been worth it. One resource that helped me was the Insight Timer app. It offers a wide range of meditations. I started with meditations of five minutes and under. Over time it became a habit. I now find myself comfortable practicing longer sessions. I also use nature as my meditation—sitting outside, listening to the birds and the wind, watching the way the light changes. It helps me reconnect with myself and slow down.

One of my most memorable meditation experiences was in Taos, New Mexico, at my aunt's house. She has a breathtaking view of the Sangre de Cristo Mountains. After a day of exploring and spending time outdoors, my aunt invited me to sit by her on the couch. She asked me to be still and just observe how the mountain changed as the sun went down. My mind calmed; my body became grounded—nothing else mattered at that moment. That moment taught me something important: Stillness doesn't have to look a certain way. Over time I've learned that there's more than one way to meditate or practice breathwork. I'm grateful that I finally discovered what works for me.

Each day I make a conscious effort to practice at least one of these habits, even if it's just for a few minutes. They have made a difference in how I handle daily stress, especially when coping with physical pain. These practices remind me that I'm not powerless when facing challenges and that each day is a gift to be grounded in. They root me in my body, clear my mind, and allow me to show up with strength and intention.

Fieldwork Reflection: What sorts of changes have you struggled to implement in your life? If your body could talk, what would it be asking for?

FIELDWORK REFLECTIONS	DATE

INSIGHTS	NOTES

NEXT STEPS

FIELDWORK REFLECTIONS	DATE

ADDITIONAL NOTES

FIELDWORK REFLECTIONS	DATE

ADDITIONAL NOTES

FIELDWORK REFLECTIONS	DATE

ADDITIONAL NOTES

FREEDOM

I am not fully healed. I am not fully wise. I am still on my way.
What matters is that I am still moving forward.

—*Yung Pueblo*, Inward

After years of inner work I finally feel myself stepping out of the cage I unknowingly built. A cage built of stress, anxiety, perfectionism, people-pleasing, and the fear of slowing down and not living. My body was exhausted from being ignored. It began to protest, screamed through pain and fatigue, and I finally found my breaking point: my health. Without my health everything changed. I couldn't move through life at the same pace. I couldn't pursue my goals, explore the world, or stay deeply connected to others in the way I once did. My body was begging me to stop. Begging me to listen, to care for it, to accept it, and to love it back. I had ignored its cries for so long, pushing through the pain and fatigue. But now I had no choice but to face my past and reality.

I didn't want to feel what I had locked away. I ran out of energy to keep running (figuratively speaking). I had no choice but to sit still and finally process the pain. I had to grieve lost dreams, my disrupted sense of safety, changed abilities, a transformed childhood, and a fractured relationship with myself. Healing required me to feel it all—deep in my bones, my nerves, my muscles.

Only then could I begin to release it. I had to learn how to calm my nervous system. I had to rebuild trust with my body and show it that it was safe now. I had to reconstruct my mind, weary and overworked from years of pushing forward without pause. I had to stop wishing my past had gone differently and begin accepting what is. This healing journey demanded consistent grit, persistent patience, and relentless courage. It has been worth enduring because I am no longer stuck in survival mode. I am finally present for the life I fought to live for.

I'm learning how to let go of the desire to control everything, because I've realized it's a losing battle. All I can control are my reactions to what happens to me and how I choose to cope and move forward with my life. The process of learning to release control and let things be as they are has softened me. I no longer live on the edge or unravel over the small stuff. Working through my past has helped me feel lighter. I'm less consumed by constant stress and anxiety. None of it holds me the way it used to. I am no longer shaking like a chihuahua, gripping everything tightly, waiting for the next thing to go wrong.

Prioritizing my mental and physical health has quieted the negative symptoms that once filled my days. One of many important lessons I have learned is accepting myself, all of me. That self-acceptance has created a space for me to show up with more patience, presence, and joy, especially in my relationship with my husband. I am no longer showing up from a place of survival. I've let go of the pressure to power walk through life, trying to reach some invisible finish line. I was raised to move fast, push hard, always achieve, but now I choose to create my own rhythm and pace. One that honors my body and my soul. Yes, I used to get annoyed by slow walkers, but now I am one. I walk like I'm retired, not rushing to get anywhere. When I can, I leave early to accommodate this slower, more intentional pace of life. I don't mind the sighs or dramatic footsteps of people rushing past me. I've let go of the need to keep up and be concerned about other people's thoughts about me.

I am still a work in progress, learning every single day. I know there will be more hard times ahead, but I also know there will be miracles, joy, and beautifully mundane days. Through it all I will continue to stay curious and observant of my life. There are moments when I catch myself slipping back into the shadow of my old cage. But then I remember what it cost me to live there, which makes me keep moving forward. On the harder days, I turn to a question I learned from *Healing Is the New High* by Vex King: "Is your intuition or trauma taking the lead?" The question resets me. It slows me down. It helps me think through my reactions and gently redirect when fear tries to take the lead. Old patterns are easy to fall into, especially when I'm tired. When I notice anxiety rising or fear looming, I know it's time to pause and examine what's really going on beneath the surface. I'm working on rewiring those automatic fear responses, choosing instead to respond with courage and compassion.

If it's late at night and I don't have the capacity to work through my buzzing thoughts, I know I just need to get some good sleep. To keep my mind from playing a loop while I try to sleep, I quickly jot down my thoughts and tell myself I can always return to them later if I still feel bothered by them. Usually, in the morning, I'll glance at them and chuckle because I can immediately identify that these were irrational thoughts, a product of being overly tired.

My past will always be a part of me. It's something I've learned to manage and accept for the rest of my life. Even though my past experiences brought me pain and changed my physical abilities, they also gave me strength, resilience, and a deeper appreciation for this life. It's a bittersweet life. Honestly, I cannot imagine who I'd be without my cancer experience and the other challenges I've faced. They changed me, but they also revealed me. I lost myself, but I am uncovering my favorite version of myself. The truest version. The highest version I was always called to be.

As I allow more of my true self to emerge, I find my spirituality growing deeper and becoming more trusting of the path I am on. I know I'll continue to evolve. The years will bring new challenges, new insights, and I'll need to adapt, again and again. My views, beliefs, and practices may shift, and my heart is open to that.

Continuously investing in myself by committing time and energy to my healing and growth has been the greatest gift I could ever give myself. I will always be in my own company, so I choose to make it great to be around. Company I can feel proud of. Company I can always feel at home with.

What I have learned on this journey is that healing for me is not about returning to exactly who I was before but becoming someone deeper, someone closer to who I was always called to be. The process is messy, exhausting, and often invisible to the outside world. But little by little it brings you home to yourself. I won't pretend this work is easy. Some days still feel heavy. Some lessons I have to relearn. But now I have the tools, support, self-compassion, and community to help me move forward. I know how to listen to myself, how to honor when I need to rest, and how to move at the pace that feels right for me mentally and physically.

I see you. You do not walk alone. I wish you the best on your journey, and may you be surrounded by love. You are valuable. You are worthy and deserving of a good life. Invest and bet on yourself. Go at your own pace. Give yourself grace when you stumble, get lost, get hurt, or have to start over. Slow down when you need to. Listen to your gut. Rest when your mind and body ask for it. Seek support. Connect with people who help you feel seen, safe, and loved. Give light to your confidence. You can be both brave and scared. Most of all, keep taking one more step.

Fieldwork Reflection: When it comes to healing, it doesn't matter how small the step as long as you take one. What's one step you can take today?

FIELDWORK REFLECTIONS	DATE

INSIGHTS	NOTES

NEXT STEPS

FIELDWORK REFLECTIONS	DATE

ADDITIONAL NOTES

FIELDWORK REFLECTIONS	DATE

ADDITIONAL NOTES

FIELDWORK REFLECTIONS	DATE

ADDITIONAL NOTES

POEMS

Healing is not linear. It's messy, unpredictable, and often happens in the smallest of moments.

—Unknown

I don't often write poetry, but when I do it comes to me in my sleep. I wake up immediately, open the Notes app on my phone, and jot it down. This happens when I'm overwhelmed by emotions. Writing these poems helps me process and heal, giving voice to feelings I struggle to express when I'm awake. Below are poems I've written throughout different times in my life. I invite you to write your own. They don't have to be perfect or follow a certain form or even make sense to anyone else. Let the words flow without judgment.

Acknowledge

After sixteen years I thought I processed you fully.
What I did do was processed at my capacity.
I did what I could.
Now I am flowing with tears and love for you.
Giving compassion.
Giving attention.
Slowing down to heal with you.

Travel light

My load is heavy.
It's time to unpack.
One by one I sit with you.
I discard.
I cherish.
I keep.
I repack what serves me now.
Leave what holds me back.

Pain

Sharp and quick,
aching and dull,
a limp in my step,
a clench in my jaw,
knots in my shoulders,
anxious thoughts running me raw,
rattling my bones—
my home haunted by fear,
searching for peace.

Grief

My body is grieving.
It aches. It twists.
It cries to release the pain.
My heart is cracked; my body is shattered.
Never before have I felt grief like you.
I've felt grief of the heart, soul, and mind.
I can't calm my body down.

It won't believe me,
that it's going to be okay.
It yearns to grieve the loss of the life inside it.
I will give my body its space and time.
I will honor it.
I will hold my body and sit in silence with it.
We will survive.

We will survive.

Anxiety and Me

Breathe with me.
When you are frightened.
Breathe with me.
When your heart races.
Breathe with me.
When your body shakes.
Breathe with me.
Hand on heart. Inhale slowly.
Exhale fully.

At Sea

Drowning in my thoughts, cast adrift in the open sea.
No land in sight, no soul nearby.
In these moments, I turn to myself—
anchored by the ways I've learned to stay afloat.

When I feel anger . . . I walk.
When I feel fear . . . I pray.
When I feel anxiety . . . I breathe.
When I feel tense . . . I dance.

When my mind is buzzing . . . I write.
When my emotions are too big . . . I step outside.
When I disassociate . . . I ground myself.
When I feel pain . . . I sit with it, then let it go.
When I feel lonely . . . I look around
remembering I'm never truly alone—
rooted with my people
and with God,
holding me steady,
grateful for their love that grounds me.

Decisions

Should I keep you?
Should I let you go?
Am I driven by fear or hope?
Here again.
Decisions to make.
Is this the right time?
Is this the best?
Is this my opinion or someone else's?
Driven by love or pain?
This time I'm driven by love.

Healing

I despised you
Ashamed of you
Angered by you
Betrayed by you
When all you needed was to be held
Needing tender love . . .

I am here now.
Holding you.
Welcoming you.
Accepting you
Embracing you.
Loving you.
For all that you are.

Together

No longer trailing behind.
No longer running ahead.
I walk alongside you.
Together.
With my head held high.
Proud to be me.

FIELDWORK REFLECTIONS	DATE

INSIGHTS	NOTES

NEXT STEPS

FIELDWORK REFLECTIONS	DATE

ADDITIONAL NOTES

FIELDWORK REFLECTIONS	DATE

ADDITIONAL NOTES

FIELDWORK REFLECTIONS	DATE

ADDITIONAL NOTES

Resources

Here I share the people, books, podcasts, and social media accounts that helped me on my healing journey. I read multiple books at once. At times, I finish the whole book; at other times, I skip around and read only certain portions. I don't always agree with everything I read in these books—or any books for that matter. I pick and choose what resonates with me. Stop, reflect, ask yourself questions, and decide what works well for you. May these resources serve you well.

Postpartum Resources

Postpartum Support International (PSI):
https://postpartum.net

PostpartumDepression.org:
https://www.postpartumdepression.org/resources/

Suicide & Crisis Lifeline:
https://988lifeline.org

Limb Loss and Limb Difference Group

Amputee Coalition:
https://amputee-coalition.org

Books

Self-Help

Breaking the Habit of Being Yourself – Joe Dispenza

Breath: The New Science of a Lost Art – James Nestor

Clarity and Connection – Yung Pueblo

Grit – Angela Duckworth

Good Vibes, Good Life: How Self-Love Is the Key to Unlocking Your Greatness – Vex King

Healing Is the New High: A Guide to Overcoming Emotional Turmoil and Finding Freedom – Vex King

Now Is the Way – Cory Allen

Power Moves – Sarah Jakes Roberts

Ready, Set, Slow – Lee Holden

Self Help: This Is Your Chance to Change Your Life – Gabrielle Bernstein

The Ayurveda Way – Anata Ripa Ajmera

The Creative Act – Rick Rubin

The Let Them Theory – Mel Robbins

Think Like a Monk – Jay Shetty

Woman Evolve – Sarah Jacksons Roberts

Cookbooks, Nutritional, and Gut Health

Cannelle et Vanille Bakes Simple: A New Way to Bake Gluten-Free (with Vegan Options for Most Recipes) – Aran Goyoaga

Eat Like a Girl: 100+ Delicious Recipes to Balance Hormones, Boost Energy, and Burn Fat – Dr. Mindy Pelz

Food Babe Kitchen – Vani Hari

Food: What the Heck Should I Eat? – Mark Hyman

The Grain Brain Cookbook – David Perlmutter

Gut: The Inside Story of Our Body's Most Underrated Organ – Giulia Enders

The Artful Way to Plant-Based Cooking: Nourishing Recipes and Heartfelt Moments – Chloé Crane-Leroux and Trudy Crane

The Glucose Goddess Method: The 4-Week Guide to Cutting Cravings, Getting Your Energy Back, and Feeling Amazing – Jessie Inchauspé

Love and Lemons Simple Feel Good Food: 125 Plant-Focused Meals to Enjoy Now or Make Ahead: A Cookbook – Jeanine Donofrio

Sweet Laurel Savory: Everyday Decadence for Whole-Food, Grain-Free Meals: A Cookbook – Laurel Gallucci and Claire Thomas

Any Ina Garten cookbooks (I adapt recipes to be gluten-free.)

Grief and End of Life

Awake at the Bedside – Paley Ellison

Bearing the Unbearable – Joanne Cacciatore

Dying Well – Ira Byock

Healing After Loss – Martha Whitmore Hickman

Signposts of Dying – Martha Jo Atkins

The Five Invitations – Frank Ostaseki

Fiction

Books I read when I needed to melt into another world.

Abby Jimenez

Just for the Summer

Life's too Short

Part of Your World

The Friend Zone

The Happily Ever After Playlist

The Situationship

Yours Truly

Emily Henry

Beach Reach

Book Lovers

Funny Story

Great Big Beautiful Life

Happy Place

People We Meet on Vacation

The Love That Split the World

Isabel Cañas

The Hacienda

The Possession of Alba Díaz

Vampires of El Norte

Rebecca Yarros

Fourth Wing

Iron Flame

Onyx Storm

Nonfiction

Braiding Sweet Grass – Robin Wall Kimmerer

The Hidden Life of Trees – Peter Wohlleben

Poetry

Home Body – Rupi Kaur

Milk and Honey – Rupi Kaur

The Sun and Her Flowers – Rupi Kaur

Podcasts

A Bit of Optimism – Simon Sinek

Unlocking Us – Brené Brown

Where Should We Begin? – Esther Perel

The School of Greatness – Lewis Howes

The Mel Robbins Podcast – Mel Robbins

Newsletters

3-2-1 Thursday – James Clear

Ozan Varol

The Brain Coach – Nawal Mustafa

Renée E. Schmachtenberger Tijerina is a childhood cancer survivor, author, and certified strengths coach. For nearly two decades she has been cancer-free, navigating life with disability, chronic illness, and the ongoing work of healing from medical trauma. Through therapy, reflection, and spiritual practice, Renée has learned how to accept her past, embrace the present, and look forward with hope.

She lives in San Antonio, Texas, with her beautiful family. *Walking Home: Journey Toward Self-Healing*, her debut book, is a heartfelt exploration of resilience, healing, and what it means to find your way after unexpected detours.